RISE

Reimagining the Resurrection Life

MORLING**PRESS**

WIPF & STOCK
An Imprint of WIPF *and* STOCK *Publishers*

RISE — REIMAGINING THE RESURRECTION LIFE
© **Morling Press and Wipf and Stock Publishers 2021**

First Published in Australia in 2021

Morling Press
122 Herring Rd, Macquarie Park NSW 2113 Australia
Phone: +61 2 9878 0201
Email: enquiries@morling.edu.au

www.morlingcollege.com/morlingpress

Wipf and Stock Publishers
199 W. 8th Ave., Suite 3
Eugene, OR 97401 United States of America

www.wipfandstock.com

ISBN: 978-0-9945726-8-4 (paperback) | 978-0-9945726-9-1 (ebook)

Designed by Impressum **www.impressum.com.au**

RISE

Reimagining the Resurrection Life

JIM BAUCOM AND ROSS CLIFFORD

An Imprint of WIPF and STOCK Publishers

For the communities of Columbia Baptist
Church and Morling College, who seek to live out
resurrection discipleship.

Contents

CONTRIBUTORS

Jim Baucom has been Senior Pastor of Columbia Church, Falls Church, Virginia, in the inner suburbs of Washington, DC, for over ten years. As a consultant, Christian leader, speaker, and writer, Dr. Baucom has worked with businesses, churches, and nonprofit organizations around the world. He has served in many leadership capacities nationally, including five years as Chairman of the Board of Trustees for the John Leland Seminary, Chairman of the Board for the Spence Leadership Network, a trustee of Averett University, and a member of the General Council of the Baptist World Alliance. He is a member of the Board of Directors for the National Association of Evangelicals, and also former Chair of the Board of Directors for Mission Alliance. Of particular importance to him is his work in the slums of Vijayawada, Andhra Pradesh, India. He holds a Bachelor of Arts degree from the University of Richmond, a Masters of Divinity from Southeastern Baptist Theological Seminary, and a Doctorate of Ministry from Princeton Theological Seminary. Dr. Baucom lives in McLean, Virginia, with his wife Debbie, and has two daughters, Marlee and Kelly.

Ross Clifford is Principal of Morling College (Seminary), Sydney. Prior to entering the Baptist ministry, he practiced as a solicitor and barrister. He was the pastor of two Sydney Baptist churches, each of which grew dramatically. He is the author of nine books including *The Cross Is Not Enough*, *Leading Lawyers' Case for the Resurrection*, *Jesus and the Gods of the New Age*, and *Beyond Prediction*. He co-pioneered outreaches into MindBodySpirit festivals. He is a former President of the Baptist Union of Australia, former President of the NSW Council of Churches, recent Chair of the Australian Lausanne Committee, past President of the Asia Pacific Baptist Federation, and was Vice President of the Baptist World Alliance from 2010 to 2015. In the Queen's Birthday Honours List of 2010 he was made a member of the Order of Australia (AM). He is married to Beverley and they have two children. His passions include legal crime novels, cricket, and all brands of football.

INTRODUCTION

Early on the first day of the week, while it was still dark, Mary Magdalene went to the tomb and saw that the stone had been removed from the entrance. So she came running to Simon Peter and the other disciple, the one Jesus loved, and said, "They have taken the Lord out of the tomb, and we don't know where they have put him!" So Peter and the other disciple started for the tomb. Both were running, but the other disciple outran Peter and reached the tomb first. He bent over and looked in at the strips of linen lying there but did not go in. Then Simon Peter came along behind him and went straight into the tomb. He

1

saw the strips of linen lying there, as well as the cloth that had been wrapped around Jesus' head. The cloth was still lying in its place, separate from the linen. Finally the other disciple, who had reached the tomb first, also went inside. He saw and believed. (They still did not understand from Scripture that Jesus had to rise from the dead.) Then the disciples went back to where they were staying. (John 20:1–9 NIV)

If the Church had contemplated the Empty Tomb as much as the Cross of its Lord, its life would have been more exhilarating and its contribution to the world more positive than has been the case.[1]

The glorious narrative of God's love for humanity unfolds like a symphony in four movements: creation, fall, redemption, and restoration. God created the world and created humanity in his image, humanity rebelled against God and lost his image, God loved humanity so much that he worked to redeem his

---

1 Beasley-Murray, "Preaching the Gospel from the Gospels," 46.

2

creation, and God has been restoring the world and his image in us ever since. Thus, the whole story of the Bible is like a beautiful musical score, the soundtrack of a love story between God and his creation, and the resurrection of Jesus Christ sets the tempo for the "rondo," the final, magnificent movement in which we now live.

Franz Joseph Haydn is widely considered as "the father of the symphony." During his career, he produced over one hundred symphonies, and his work served as a compositional model for those who came behind him. Haydn somehow managed to capture the rhythm of creation in his work, and audiences have resonated ever since. In the Greek, the word *symphonia* translates as an "agreement or concord of sound," and, indeed, something in the symphony strikes a chord with the human experience of life. Though there are many symphonies, and each of them is in some way unique, all of them are similar in compositional tenor. Each begins with an "allegro," a rapid, exciting introduction to the score, after which each descends into an "adagio," a slow melancholic counter to the opening. The third movement of every true symphony is a "minuet" or

3

"scherzo," an invitation to shuck off the sadness of the "adagio" and dance. The final movement of the symphony is the "rondo," a rejoinder that recaptures the theme of the opening "allegro" and closes the symphony in the rapturous splendor of re-creation. Lovers of symphony know exactly what to expect when they sit before a great orchestra and await its opening scores.

This is the rhythm of life as the Bible describes it and as we experience it. Like the opening score of a symphony, there is the booming allegro with all of its splendor, the moment when God creates humanity in his image:

> Then God said, "Let us make mankind in our image, in our likeness, so that they may rule over the fish in the sea and the birds in the sky, over the livestock and all the wild animals, and over all the creatures that move along the ground." So God created mankind in his own image, in the image of God he created them; male and female he created them. (Gen 1:26–27 NIV)

And then there is the soul-crushing adagio of humanity's fall from God's grace:

> When the woman saw that the fruit of the tree
> was good for food and pleasing to the eye, and
> also desirable for gaining wisdom, she took some
> and ate it. She also gave some to her husband,
> who was with her, and he ate it. Then the eyes
> of both of them were opened, and they realized
> they were naked; so they sewed fig leaves
> together and made coverings for themselves.
> (Gen 3:6–7 NIV)

Were this a sonata comprised of only these two movements, there would be little to applaud. Indeed, many exit the hall of life's symphony at this intermission, but this production is only half completed.

Just as we are left to despair, in rushes the third movement of creation's symphony, the scherzo of Christ's cross, the Creator's invitation to dance again.

> Yes, Adam's one sin brings condemnation for
> everyone, but Christ's one act of righteousness
> brings a right relationship with God and new
> life for everyone. Because one person disobeyed
> God, many became sinners. But because one
> other person obeyed God, many will be made

5

righteous. God's law was given so that all people could see how sinful they were. But as people sinned more and more, God's wonderful grace became more abundant. So just as sin ruled over all people and brought them to death, now God's wonderful grace rules instead, giving us right standing with God and resulting in eternal life through Jesus Christ our Lord. (Rom 5:18–21 NLT)

And finally, the symphony of life is completed in the resurrection rondo, the opportunity of re-creation.

But because of his great love for us, God, who is rich in mercy, made us alive with Christ even when we were dead in transgressions— it is by grace you have been saved. And God raised us up with Christ and seated us with him in the heavenly realms in Christ Jesus. (Eph 2:4–6 NIV)

Indeed, the resurrection of Jesus Christ is a magnificent, rollicking rejoinder to the primary creative theme performance.

In light of this complete symphony, why are humans made in the image of God now so unfamiliar with their Creator or his image? This is a question far more difficult to grapple with than that of God's existence. It is relatively easy for us to conjecture that there must be a Creator, an uncaused first cause, an initiator, a divine designer. But if he exists, then surely, we must implicate either him or ourselves in explaining a radical disconnect between us. Neither is a simple task. To implicate him is to know a life of abandonment, but to implicate ourselves could elicit a life of shame. Perhaps the essence of atheism or agnosticism is the avoidance of these negative emotions.

Unfortunately, modern Christianity often fails to resolve this dilemma, as many atheistic antagonists rightly observe. In our view, the problem is that many Christians and churches today remain past the intermission, but still depart before the final rondo of the resurrection. The irony is that those followers of Christ who would most claim to love God are often also those who provoke the most shame. After all, shame is a powerful short-term motivator, though it seldom provides the impetus for lasting change. Too often, such messages overshadow the good news ("gospel") of God's real story and undermine the power of human response to God's astounding love. This accentuation of human shame and a subsequent search for its remedy lead to a centering of the Christian message in the cross of Christ. The scherzo of Christ's cross and its promise of forgiveness alone cannot possibly complete creation's symphony. The resurrection of Jesus is far too frequently a happy postlude to a cathartic chorus left unresolved and the hearer is left untransformed and discontented.

Despite what many would lead us to believe, the full symphony of creation played out in the Bible is neither one of abandonment nor of shame, but rather one of re-creation and restoration. The Scriptures do reveal a Creator God who rightly judges the creation to have walked away from him, but also a Creator who lovingly pursues his creation in order to redeem it. We believe that what humans often experience as emptiness and loneliness—an experience of being lost—is really a deep desire to be restored, even re-created in God's image. We believe that human beings long for the completion of the rondo of the resurrection.

To be clear, we are not saying that the cross is ineffectual. If we understand the Bible correctly, precisely the opposite is true: the cross of Christ is the indispensable prelude to the re-creating chorus of the resurrected Lord, the postlude being the very presence of God's Spirit. In time, the Scriptures also assure us that the encore will be the creation of a "new heaven and a new earth" (Rev 21:1). The cross is essential, of course, because its forgiveness erases the stain of sin and produces a *tabula rasa* ("blank slate") upon which God can rewrite his image. But the cross of Christ is not the re-creation for which we humans so yearn; alone, it does not restore God's creation. It is the resurrection of Jesus that restores humanity according to the Creator's divine design and regenerates God's image within us. The resurrection of Jesus Christ is the hope of the world and the answer to humanity's deepest longings!

Yet, we are tempted to settle for mere forgiveness and momentary satiations of shallow cravings. We seem entirely unaware that this hunger springs from our most essential desire to reacquire the true image of God. We are duped into believing that, once forgiven; we can yet be satisfied if we consume enough of creation's "blessings" without being restored fully to the

Creator. That will never be enough! As the seventeenth-century mathematician and philosopher Pascal astutely observed:

> What else does this craving, and this helplessness, proclaim but that there was once in man a true happiness, of which all that now remains is the empty print and trace? This he tries in vain to fill with everything around him, seeking in things that are not there the help he cannot find in those that are, though none can help, since this infinite abyss can be filled only with an infinite and immutable object; in other words by God himself.[2]

Perhaps more simply, the great African church father Augustine introduced his *Confessions* writing to God, "You have made us for yourself, and our hearts are restless till they find their rest in you." We are tempted to settle for less than Christ's resurrection, but only resurrection will do!

Even if we are trying to be good children of the heavenly Father, we are also tempted to settle for a slightly more subtle version of Pharisaical legalism in the shadow of the cross. In this

---

2 Pascal, *Pensees*, 45.

instance, we speak the law with a softer voice in Jesus's name, but we do not have a clue about the liberty of abundant life in the risen Lord. As Ross frequently says, "If I get beat up at church one more time, I will crawl back into the tomb." As Jim frequently tells his church family, "People become what you tell them they are, not what you tell them they should be." Symbol of God's grace that it is, many have nonetheless used the cross of Jesus as a whipping post for naughty people, beating even the redeemed with the cords of shame. The empty tomb and presence of the risen Lord in the Holy Spirit tell us who we are and whose we are. The resurrection is nothing if not hopeful and restorative, evoking joy in the life of both believer and church.

In this book, we attempt to understand the hopeful and restorative course back to God's design for human life through the resurrection of Jesus Christ. We do this by tracing the cartography of the Bible both for God's original creation and for Christ's resurrection re-creation. We hope to not only demonstrate what the new creation looks like and describe how we might live in it joyously, but also to demonstrate that humans are desperately seeking the rondo of resurrection life. Further, we believe that those who hear the full symphony of God's creation are ushered into a life of joyful abundance. We will demonstrate that the resurrection enjoins a clear response to live as new creatures that the cross alone cannot engender. This is the resurrection rondo!

CHAPTER 1:

BACK TO THE GARDEN

The Son is the image of the invisible God, the firstborn over all creation. For in him all things were created: things in heaven and on earth, visible and invisible, whether thrones or powers or rulers or authorities; all things have been created through him and for him. He is before all things, and in him all things hold together. (Col 1:15–17 NIV)

Who can explain the secret pathos of Nature's loveliness? It is a touch of melancholy inherited from our mother Eve. It is an unconscious memory of the lost Paradise. It is the sense that even if we should find another Eden, we would not be fit to enjoy it perfectly nor stay in it forever.[3]

The apostle Paul speaks of resurrection re-creation in Romans 4:25 at the heart of his systematic theology: "[Jesus] was delivered over to death for our sins and was raised to life for our justification." So, the purpose of Jesus's death was to clean the slate by providing for the forgiveness of human sinfulness and self-centeredness, but it was Christ's resurrection that redrew God's image on the *tabula rasa* of the human soul.

That was God's intention all along. What good is an erased board unless it is to be written anew? The primary emphasis must always be on what has been found, not on what has been lost, on what has been restored rather than on what has been

---

3 Van Dyke, "VIII, Au Large," 11.

broken, and on that which has been re-created, not on what has been demolished. Otherwise, we will forever live either as blemished or emptied, rather than re-created and filled. In order that we fully understand this truth, we must go back to the very beginning, back to the garden.

The Lost Garden

The Bible presents the facts of God's creation of earth and its inhabitants in two concurrent dramatic acts, the first poetic and the second narrative. The first act, found primarily in Genesis 1, is centered in the identity of the Creator. The second, found primarily in Genesis 2, is centered in the experience of the created. The Genesis 2 narrative is set in the garden of Eden, a perfect place in which human beings exist in complete harmony with God, each other, and the rest of the created order. All of Eden is a reflection of God's love, and the man and woman are the pinnacle of creation. They joyfully tend the garden with full reign over it except for one tree from which they must not eat that of the "knowledge of good and evil." The first human pair know nothing of evil, so all that they undertake is good and perfectly aligned with the will of their Creator. Theirs is a utopian existence entailing right thought, right action, and right relationship.

God's ultimate love is shown to the man and woman most absolutely though, in that they are given free will mirroring God's own autonomy. Scripture is clear that God knew when creating them that humans would choose their own way over that of the Creator. The first act of "sin" or rebellion against God is thus presented as an act of selfish consumption. The man and woman take what they want without regard to consequence by eating from the tree of the knowledge of good and evil. There is a vain attempt to become all-knowing, and thus gods, themselves. In so doing, they scuttle not only their idyllic relationship with the Creator but also their harmonious existence with each other and the rest of creation. In essence, they defile the image of God (historically known in the church as the *imago Dei*) created within them so that they no longer resonate with the perfectly melodious mission of God (or *missio Dei*). They lose their identity as images of God, keepers of the garden, and stewards of God's creation, and they pass their spiritual amnesia on to their offspring.

This, then, is the state in which we now exist: as warped images of God out of alignment with God's divine design. We are people out of relationship with the Creator and entirely out of rhythm with the creation. This is the condition known to traditional theology as "original sin," a condition perpetuated in each successive generation of humans in our quest for autonomy and our thirst for consumption. We can never satisfy our deepest desires to recover the image of our Creator and relationship with him, but that does not stop us from trying. The great deception we now believe is that having enough of the creation will bring us back to the Creator. The truth is that we only deepen our relational breach with God by idolizing ourselves as possessors of the creation.

The biggest movie of 1997, by far, was Titanic, which debuted around the eighty-fifth anniversary of one of the modern world's most famous disasters. Apart from the far-fetched love story, what most fascinated viewers was the historical backdrop of the unsinkable ship meeting its demise with 2,224 mostly

17

well-heeled passengers aboard. More than 1,500 of those passengers "went down with the ship."

The 883-foot Titanic departed Southampton, England, on April 10, 1912, for its maiden voyage. It was the largest passenger ship ever built and considered by many also as the best engineered. Carefully designed with a sturdy hull, powerful engines, and an interior labyrinth of sealable compartments, the ship was thought virtually unsinkable. The most luxurious cruise of all time delighted its passengers as it made port stops for fuel in France and Ireland and then headed west for New York. But on April 14, at 11:40 p.m., the ship grazed a large iceberg 375 miles south of Newfoundland and took a long gash in its hull. It took less than three hours for the massive luxury liner to break apart and fall into the icy sea. Only 750 passengers survived, partly because there were only life rafts on board to accommodate half of them. At 11:39, happy cruisers had been living the high life: resigned to luxury cabins, dining in fine restaurants stocked with expensive wines, reading in the ship's library, working out in its gymnasium, or swimming in its indoor pool. Then at 11:40, everything suddenly changed.

One can never read the first four chapters of Genesis without feeling a Titanic kick in the gut. God's design for our world was so very perfect, so pleasing, so delightful. It all changed in an instant the moment sin and rebellion entered the world by human decision. We understand that God gave the first human pair free will when he created them in his image, and we do not really fault them their rebellion. Any of us would have done the same thing. In fact, we have been actively participating in the tragedy of original sin ever since. We just keep eating the same apple again and again! But we do mourn what was lost and long for its restoration. We long for the true image of our Creator.

We are utterly lost, but we are not stupid, and so we desperately desire to get "back to the garden." In the Joni Mitchell hit Woodstock made famous by Crosby, Stills, and Nash, the chorus opines, "We are stardust," caught in the devil's plan, "and we've got to get ourselves back to the garden." But we cannot restore what has been broken of our own accord. We cannot get ourselves back to the paradise of Eden by our own effort, and we never could. What has been lost is the very image of the Creator, and only the Creator can re-create that image within us.

The Last Adam

Enter the "last Adam," as the apostle Paul calls him, Jesus Christ. Enter the new creation! In 1 Corinthians 15, the Bible's "resurrection chapter," Paul recounts God's amazing plan to get us "back to the garden."

> So it is written: "The first man Adam became a living being"; the last Adam, a life-giving spirit. The spiritual did not come first, but the natural, and after that the spiritual. The first man was of the dust of the earth; the second man is of heaven. As was the earthly man, so are those who are of the earth; and as is the heavenly man, so also are those who are of heaven. And just as we have borne the image of the earthly man, so shall we bear the image of the heavenly man. (1 Cor 15:45–49 NIV)

Many followers of Jesus have looked at this passage and thought it more a reference to the afterlife than anything else. "Of

20

course," they have surmised, "we have borne the image of the earthly Adam in this life, but in the next, surely we will bear the image of the heavenly man." They have missed the point entirely! As the last Adam, Jesus has already ushered in a new Eden. This is why Paul is able to write elsewhere, "Therefore, if anyone is in Christ, the new creation has come: The old *has gone*, the new *is here!*" (2 Cor 5:17, italics added).

The new is here and now, not just waiting to be experienced in the future. Followers of Jesus who have identified with his death in order to know his resurrection are already residents of the new Eden. They will live with God and bear his image for eternity!

This is the oft-missed good news of the New Testament: the new is already here! As the last Adam, Jesus is both the present Creator and the prototypical image of creation as it was intended to be from the beginning. In the first instance, John writes:

> In the beginning was the Word [Jesus], and the
> Word was with God, and the Word was God. He
> was with God in the beginning. Through him

all things were made; without him nothing was
made that has been made. (John 1:1–3 NIV)

In other words, Jesus is, from the beginning, the creative force of God in the universe. And yet, in the second instance, Jesus was the standard of creation while he lived on earth. He was the living, breathing paradigm of humanity as it was intended to be. So, the apostle Paul writes in Philippians 2:

[Jesus,] being in very nature God, did not consider equality with God something to be used to his own advantage; rather, he made himself nothing by taking the very nature of a servant, being made in human likeness. And being found in appearance as a man, he humbled himself by becoming obedient to death—even death on a cross! (Phil 2:6–8 NIV)

Though perfect in nature and in complete harmony with the divine design of creation, Jesus lived among us as a human being in order to demonstrate the real possibility of life as God had intended it to be. As Athanasius of Alexandria proclaimed in the early fourth century, "He became like us in order that we might become like him."

Again, perhaps it is this profound mystery that has led to such an overemphasis on the cross of Christ and such an underemphasis on Christ's resurrection. The problem is that the cross is nothing apart from the resurrection. Anyone could die (and all do), but only Jesus could be raised from the dead and then exalted to the right hand of the Father. This is why Paul concludes his thought in Philippians 2:

> Therefore God exalted him to the highest place and gave him the name that is above every name, that at the name of Jesus every knee should bow, in heaven and on earth and under the earth, and every tongue acknowledge that Jesus Christ is Lord, to the glory of God the Father. (Phil 2:9–11 NIV)

It is through his resurrection that Christ is exalted, and we are restored to God's divine design in creation. It is in the resurrection that we discover our purpose for being, by rediscovering God's image in our lives. Our hearts long for resurrection transformation and a return to creation's garden!

Transformation

Deeply rooted in the human soul is a yearning to recover what has been lost and to rediscover the beauty of the garden. We desperately want to recover a passion for life itself. The apostle Paul famously counsels followers of Jesus: "Do not be conform to the pattern of this world, but be transformed by the renewing of your mind. Then you will be able to test and approve what God's will is—his good, pleasing and perfect will" (Rom 12:2 NIV). What Paul means by this is that we should not maintain the form of the fallen world of sin and shame, but instead receive the transformation of the risen Lord and take our place in the new creation. The resurrection is transformational!

Within the modern Western literature of leadership, James MacGregor Burns is credited with having introduced the contemporary concept of "transformational leadership" in his 1978 work simply entitled "Leadership." Burns's ideas are fairly complex, but the essence of his thought is that there is a big difference between simple transaction and lasting transformation. We all conduct transactions every day, of course.

We share information, pay bills, purchase products, and the like, because we have to in order to survive and thrive. Contractual interactions like these are the stock and trade of civilization: you do something for me, and I will do something for you. We cannot avoid them.

The question is whether or not our whole lives have become a series of transactions. Genesis presents the first human sin as a transaction of consumption. The woman and her husband each eat from the forbidden tree of the knowledge of good and evil when tempted to become just like God. From that moment on, humans have existed primarily as transactional creatures acting in their own self-interest. The question that governs attitude and behavior in this order of our own creation is, "What's in it for me?" The reason most people are what Burns describes as transactional is because it works, at least in the short term. But we were not created for this, and so we long for more. We hunger for transformation, to exist for something greater than our limited lives. We need for our transactions to serve some greater transformation.

God's loving response to the transactional world we cling to has been to transform it through transformed leaders. Abraham's God-given vision was to found a new nation, a place where his descendants would live united around their monotheistic religious practice, concern for those less fortunate, and justice before a righteous God. Moses's patient leadership transformed a frightened bunch of slaves into a kingdom force ready to reoccupy the promised land. Joshua inspired unsure people by symbol and example to trust God and work together to claim a land flowing with milk and honey. King David transformed an inconsequential nation into a mighty force by bringing disparate tribes together around common values and aspirations. Nehemiah stood out in a crowd of despotic leaders as one more concerned with the good of the people than his own wealth and fame, and brought people together around a common vision of rebuilding a wall and a holy city. Ezra reestablished temple worship and rallied the people around the forgotten Torah, helping them to see themselves again as God's people. All of these leaders called the people to something greater than themselves, and that's what they longed for. These people wanted to recover the image of God.

When confronted by Christ on the road to Damascus, the apostle Paul traded his role in a transactional religious system for a transformational philosophy as he served people whose lives were changed. He helped Timothy to develop into a church leader who, according to tradition, died for his faith a respected pastor. Onesimus, a runaway slave, became Paul's beloved partner in the gospel. John Mark changed dramatically from an immature and fragile young man to a valuable member of Paul's evangelistic team. Paul was a transformational leader.

But, of course, the ultimate transformational life and leader was found in Jesus. Jesus never simply transacted business as usual, and he resisted any attempts by those around him to be anything other than transformative. After choosing a transformational symbol in baptism to inaugurate his public ministry, Jesus was led by the Spirit into the wilderness for forty days of prayer and fasting. In the wilderness, the devil tempted Jesus to settle for a transaction on three occasions. These three temptations involved offers of provision, prestige, and power, respectively. Jesus responded transformationally to each of the devil's attempts at a transaction by quoting words from Deuteronomy 6–8, the very heart of God's standard for his creation. He simply refused to capitulate. When he returned, he approached men transacting their everyday business and invited them to enter into a transformational journey as his disciples. He offered them nothing in return except an opportunity to be transformed and to transform the lives of others.

This pattern of transformational initiative and response defined Jesus's leadership at every turn. When the woman at the well kept trying to transact business with Jesus, he transformed the conversation from physical water to spiritual living water and from ritual to true worship. He counseled his followers not to lay up treasures and worry about them (transact), but instead to store away heavenly treasure and trust God's provision (transform). He warned them not to use prayer and fasting as earthly transactions to be seen by others, but to seek their heavenly Father's heart in private instead. There are so many examples that we could exhaust an entire volume referencing them, but Jesus's conversation with Nicodemus in John 3 is especially rich.

When the Pharisee Nicodemus visited Jesus, he came as a chief representative of a highly transactional religious system (think Sabbath laws). Even the secretive manner in which he approached Jesus in the dark of night indicates that his intent was transactional. Nicodemus marveled at the signs Jesus was performing, and he wanted to ascertain whether this miracle worker was a threat to his way of life. Jesus discerned that the Pharisee's interest was mostly transactional, and he responded to him transformationally: "No one can see the kingdom of God unless they are born again" (v. 3). Jesus was obviously speaking about transformation. Nicodemus did not understand Jesus, so he kept pressing for a transaction: "How can someone be born when they are old? Surely they cannot enter a second time into their mother's womb to be born!" (v. 4). Jesus would not bite but continued his transformational line saying one must be born from above, of the Spirit; that the Spirit operates mysteriously, transformationally. Nicodemus just could not get it, because he could not break his transactional mold: "How can this possibly be?" This made no sense to him at all. Through his transactional lens, he simply could not understand what Jesus was offering.

In this interaction with Nicodemus, Jesus provided a basic distinction between transaction and transformation: "Flesh gives birth to flesh, but the Spirit gives birth to spirit." In other words, one transaction leads to another, and it takes an intervention from God to change that. In the best known of all biblical passages, Jesus is recorded as finally telling Nicodemus, "God so loved the world that he gave his one and only Son, that whoever believes in him shall not perish but have eternal life. For God did not send his Son into the world to condemn the world, but to save the world through him" (John 3:16–17 NIV).

Like Nicodemus, we are prone to see God's redemptive work in Jesus through a transactional lens, so we highlight the forgiveness attained in the cross. We rightly acknowledge that Jesus paid the price for our sins in his crucifixion, but we wrongly end the story with that "transaction." Yes, we believe that the cross of Jesus is transformational, but that is not how we often hear it proclaimed. As important as forgiveness is, those in the culture around us beg to know if this is all there is. More pointedly, what transformation is served by the transaction of the cross? The answer comes, of course, in the resurrection: the restoration of God's creation. Indeed, the cross and resurrection are really one single expression of God's grace. Neither makes any sense without the other. We are forgiven in order to be restored. Heeding the prompting of the Holy Spirit to identify with Jesus's cross and die to ourselves is work that we must do continually. But re-creation is work that only the new gardener, the resurrected Lord, can accomplish in our lives.

The New Gardener

In the resurrection of Jesus Christ, God is restoring his creation garden and bidding us to enter it. The last Adam is the new gardener, and we are being invited to till, plant, and cultivate with him! This imagery is present throughout the New Testament, but we often miss it while reading through our transactional lens. In fact, this imagery is hidden in plain view in John's account of the first Easter:

Now Mary stood outside the tomb crying. As she wept, she bent over to look into the tomb and saw two angels in white, seated where Jesus' body had been, one at the head and the other at the foot. They asked her, "Woman, why are you crying?" "They have taken my Lord away," she said, "and I don't know where they have put him." At this, she turned around and saw Jesus standing there, but she did not realize that it was Jesus. He asked her, "Woman, why are you crying? Who is it you are looking for?" Thinking he was the gardener, she said, "Sir, if you have carried him away, tell me where you have put him, and I will get him." Jesus said to her, "Mary." She turned toward him and cried out in Aramaic, "Rabboni!" (which means "Teacher"). Jesus said, "Do not hold on to me, for I have not yet ascended to the Father. Go instead to my brothers and tell them, 'I am ascending to my Father and your Father, to my God and your God.'" (John 20:11–17 NIV)

Could Mary's first impression that the risen Lord was the gardener be more than a simple misunderstanding?

What are the chances that Mary would not otherwise recognize Jesus on that first Easter morning? Mary Magdalene traveled with Jesus as one of his closest followers. She was present at Jesus's two most important moments: the crucifixion and the resurrection. Within the four Gospels, she is named at least twelve times, more than most of Jesus's apostles. In the New Testament, Jesus cleansed her of "seven demons" and made her well. Her life was utterly and completely transformed by the Messiah. When Jesus was crucified, Mary Magdalene was there supporting him in his final moments and mourning his death, even after all of the other disciples except John had fled. She was present at his burial. She is the person that the Gospels indicate as the first to realize that Jesus had risen and to testify to that central teaching of faith. Augustine quoted earlier sources in the church in calling her the "apostle to the apostles." No one knew Jesus better than Mary Magdalene! It is inconceivable that Mary would not have recognized Jesus, even considering her state of shock at the open doorway to the empty tomb.

The remarkable revelation of John 20 is that Mary is the first to behold the new gardener. As such, the risen Lord stands before her with a spiritual aura so overwhelming it cannot be fully apprehended by the bodily senses. Jesus even cautions her not to hold him in this state. While resurrected in the flesh, Jesus has begun the spiritual process of restoring the garden of creation. This is the reality upon which Paul reflects in 1 Corinthians 15:45–49 when he refers to the last Adam, the risen Lord, as a "life-giving spirit" and "heavenly man." This heavenly man is the new gardener of the new creation. He is the grand re-creator!

We have already referenced the beginning of John's Gospel and its connection to the creation of the world. Actually, the entirety of the Fourth Gospel casts the incarnation of God in Christ within the context of creation. It should come as no surprise that John presents Jesus from start to finish as the one who has come to restore that which he created. His purpose is not only to rescue humans from the fall, but to re-imprint his image on their souls. This closing introduction to the new gardener should come as no surprise, then (though somehow it does). Just as John begins the Gospel narrative with the creation

("In the beginning . . ."), he completes it with the new gardener's re-creation.

John does not merely end his story with Mary's recognition of the great restorer. Having seen the risen Lord, the apostle to the apostles goes straightaway to the twelve with the remarkable news. That very evening, they miraculously behold the re-creator for themselves:

> Mary Magdalene went to the disciples with the news: "I have seen the Lord!" And she told them that he had said these things to her. On the evening of that first day of the week, when the disciples were together, with the doors locked for fear of the Jewish leaders, Jesus came and stood among them and said, "Peace be with you!" After he said this, he showed them his hands and side. The disciples were overjoyed when they saw the Lord. Again Jesus said, "Peace be with you! As the Father has sent me, I am sending you." And with that he breathed on them and said, "Receive the Holy Spirit." (John 20:18–22 NIV)

The typical reader puzzles over the manner in which Jesus gives the apostles the resurrection presence of the Holy Spirit, missing entirely the risen Lord's first act of re-creation. The new gardener breathes on them.

Genesis 2:7 describes the creation of man with this sentence: "Then the Lord God formed a man from the dust of the ground and breathed into his nostrils the breath of life, and the man became a living being." It is by the giving of his own spirit, the "breath of life," that God animates dirt to establish his image within his creation. And it is with his breath that the risen Lord reanimates his followers to reestablish his image in the new creation. It is this same Holy Spirit that manifests on the day of Pentecost when the church of Jesus Christ is born.

The risen Lord is present in the world still through the indwelling Holy Spirit, and he beckons us into the garden of the new creation. His invites us to passionately incarnate anew the image of God for which we were designed "in the beginning." Paul's words in Ephesians 5:14 seem an apropos expression of this rich invitation: "Wake up, sleeper, rise from the dead, and Christ will shine on you." In order for us to awaken to what it means to live in this restored garden, we must recognize what has been lost in the fall of humanity. We must know what has been lost in order to find it. And so, we must comprehend fully what life was like in the first garden. We must seek the original divine design of the gardener for all dimensions of our lives to realize the immensity of what has occurred in the resurrection.

CHAPTER 2:

SHAME

This is how God showed his love among us: He sent his one and only Son into the world that we might live through him. This is how we know that we live in him and he in us: He has given us of his Spirit. And we have seen and testify that the Father has sent his Son to be the Savior of the world. If anyone acknowledges that Jesus is the Son of God, God lives in them and they in God. And so we know and rely on the love God has for us. God is love. Whoever lives in love lives in God, and God in them. This is how love is made complete among us so that we will have confidence on the day of judgment: In this world we are like Jesus. There is no fear in love. But perfect love drives out fear. (1 John 4:9, 13–18a NIV)

Shame was an emotion he had abandoned years earlier. Addicts know no shame. You disgrace yourself so many times you become immune to it.[4]

If you have a garden, a yard, or anything of the sort, you do not like weeds. Webster defines a weed as "a plant that is not of value where it is growing and is usually of vigorous growth; especially one that tends to overgrow or choke out more desirable plants." In my endless quest for a perfect Virginia yard, I feel like I am in a perpetual war on weeds, which blow in from neighboring yards and try to invade my well-tended crop of Kentucky tall fescue. I have pulled them, sprayed them, pelleted them, poisoned them, you name it. I've done everything but blow them out of the ground, and if someone shows me that will get rid of them, I'll probably do that, too. I hate weeds!

---

4 This quote is attributed to Grisham, *The Testament.*

Basically, there are two ways to treat weeds: one can spot treat them or address them more broadly. In the former instance, it is like playing whack-a-mole: the minute you have treated one the next one is under your foot. If a yard is bad enough, there is not really much one can do but kill the whole lawn and start over. That is the advice a neighbor of mine was given by a lawn expert a couple of weeks ago. Round it up in August and replant or sod in September. He was not happy, nor did he follow the advice! He still has a yard full of weeds.

Once one gets a healthy lawn, the best way to ward off weeds is actually to grow plenty of thick, healthy grass, mow it higher, and leave as little room for pervasive plants as possible. That means aerating and planting new seed every single fall and following a consistent maintenance regimen. A few years ago, I finally had the perfect stand of tall fescue. Then my lawn was attacked by grubs, and the whole thing was ruined. I had to roll the entire thing up, literally, in September, and start over. It was miserable! The one thing I hate more than weeds is white grubs. Weeds and grubs are the bane of my existence, thorns in my flesh to remind me of my mortal limitations. Every year, I think of God's word to humanity in Genesis 3:17–18: "Cursed is the ground because of you . . . it will produce thorns and thistles for you." Weeds and grubs are a reminder to me of shame.

Shame is the true bane of our existence, the pervasive and vigorously growing quantity of no value whatever that chokes out abundant life. There is the mild shame we all grow up with, of course. We swear we will never in turn shame our own children, but we do. One person has usually shamed another already before they even realize they have; that is how pervasive shame is. Once my daughters went off to college, I always looked forward to their visits home. Inevitably, they showed up to tell me that they had plans laid out for the entire weekend and that I would not see them much. Before I could catch myself, I was saying things I had heard my parents say to me: "Well, we're glad to pay for college, but we were hoping for a little gratitude once in a while. And that car you are driving belongs to me, and it is not cheap. And your mother is making your favorite meal. But that's okay, we understand, you go on and have a good time with your friends." You know the lines.

Then there is the more pernicious shame that Satan uses to keep us at a distance from God. The embarrassment about failures, stupid things we have done or said, and our weaknesses. Shame drives a wedge between us and God as well as between us and others, but that does not stop us from planting new shame weeds in our life lawns every day. In fact, the problem is so severe that we can spot treat until the world spins down and it will not come close to attacking the problem. The garden of this world is so choked off with shame weeds and eaten up with sin grubs that we need a whole new start.

And that is precisely what God has done for us in Christ's cross and resurrection. The cross is so replete with forgiveness that it destroys sin and shame once for all for anyone willing to accept Jesus's death as their own. And the resurrection is the planting of a whole new garden, an entirely fresh creation. God's plan in creation was never that those created in his image should live in shame, and that is not his intention for your life now!

Shamelessness in the First Garden —First Movement

God created humanity to know no shame. The first human pair did not even require an understanding of good and evil, because they were created to live in perfect harmony with God's plan. They were not only sinless, but shameless, just as Genesis 2:25 states: "Adam and his wife were both naked, and they felt no shame." Imagine that, standing in the garden in their birthday suits and knowing nothing different than that they should be. In the Genesis creation narrative, nudity is a symbol of shameless authenticity. The man and his wife were naked before God and each other, and they had no reason to be embarrassed. They were transparently accessible to God, to themselves, and to each other, and they were utterly at peace.

The creation account portrays humans as the pinnacle of God's creation and uniquely afforded free will, both the capacity and liberty to decide for themselves.

Without this freedom, humans cannot possibly be bearers of God's image, since he is entirely unbounded and infinitely free. Neither does Genesis depict a Creator who stands over the shoulders of his children, monitoring everything they do like some helicopter parent. If God stands over them all of the time, they cannot exercise their freedom and incarnate his image fully. They must explore, learn, and grow independently as they experience the garden and each other. The Creator leaves them to tend and discover the garden with playful delight, and he comes to visit with them from time to time. Evidently, God often stops by the garden to spend time with them "in the cool of the day" (Gen 3:8). He comes around like a loving parent in the evening, eager to hear of his children's adventures through the day.

It is surely impossible for us even to conceive of this first garden entirely devoid of shame. The Hebrew word translated "shame" in Genesis 2:25 is *bosh*, the same word from which we get the English word abashed. This Hebrew term implies a feeling of insignificance before another. For most healthy people, nakedness is no real issue unless there is someone present to witness it. Even when we are uncomfortable beholding ourselves in bathroom mirrors, it is because we are consumed with how we stack up against other people. Then the fear of comparison creeps in. In the garden, the man and his wife are not concerned with how they compare to one another, or even with how they compare to God. A good way to restate Genesis 2:25 would be, "Adam and his wife were both uncovered, and they did not feel the least bit inadequate."

Before sin enters the world, any impulse is a good and right fulfillment of God's design for his creation. The man and the woman do not need to think twice about what they desire, and they do not second guess anything they do. They are single-minded, and one of them has the same inclinations as the other. They are both inclined to God and the beauty of his creation. They want for nothing they do not have, so they have no emotions they do not want. And yet, also difficult for us to conceive is that there is some impulse inherent in their free will to wish for something more. And in that impulse is the seed of the fall.

Shamelessness Lost
—Second Movement

Many of us are quite familiar with the story of the fall found in Genesis 3.

> Now the serpent was more crafty than any of the wild animals the Lord God had made. He said to the woman, "Did God really say, 'You must not eat from any tree in the garden'?"
>
> The woman said to the serpent, "We may eat fruit from the trees in the garden, but God did say, 'You must not eat fruit from the tree that is in the middle of the garden, and you must not touch it, or you will die.'" "You will not certainly die," the serpent said to the woman. "For God knows that when you eat from it your eyes will be opened, and you will be like God, knowing good and evil."
>
> When the woman saw that the fruit of the tree was good for food and pleasing to the eye, and also desirable for gaining wisdom, she took some and ate it. She also gave some to her husband, who was with her, and he ate

it. Then the eyes of both of them were opened and they realized they were naked; so they sewed fig leaves together and made coverings for themselves.

Then the man and his wife heard the sound of the Lord God as he was walking in the garden in the cool of the day, and they hid from the Lord God among the trees of the garden. But the Lord God called to the man, "Where are you?" He answered, "I heard you in the garden, and I was afraid because I was naked; so, I hid." And he said, "Who told you that you were naked? Have you eaten from the tree that I commanded you not to eat from?" (Gen 3:1–11 NIV)

We tend to oversimplify this story of humanity's rebellion against God and fall from grace in ways that do not serve us well. We read the chronicle and distill it into a simple morality tale: Adam and Eve did what God told them not to, and now they get what is coming to them. The narrative is actually so much richer, in fact, frighteningly so. To understand the story fully, we need to investigate the presence of "the tree of the knowledge of good and evil" in the garden of creation. What is it, and why is it so conveniently accessible at the garden's center? We do not like to ponder such questions, because they cause us to wonder whether God entices the first human pair to sin, like leaving forbidden candy in front of children. What does God think will happen? We read the narrative and recognize that we probably would have eaten the prohibited fruit, too. We would all be "bad."

But that tree has to be where it is in the garden, else Adam and Eve do not really possess free will akin to God's. Removing an object of temptation from our grasp is often a good idea, but it does not change our actual capacity to choose it. If there is nothing present in the garden that can be chosen against God's will, then there is no real liberty. And that tree represents the one thing the man and his wife do not already have that could possibly be desired, the very thing God has withheld from them for their own good. The fruit of that tree will imbue them with a knowledge of things God never intended they require, an awareness of evil.

When the serpent tells the woman that the fruit will make her equal to God, and she sees that it looks especially pleasing, she eats it. Her husband is right there with her and makes no effort to prevent it. Then he joins in without reservation. "The eyes of both are opened" at the same time and suddenly they see the world very differently, beginning with the way in which they see themselves. They realize that they are naked, and for the first time they feel inadequate. This is the essence of shame and its emotional expression, fear.

The problem is that humans are not designed by God to accommodate this kind of moral and ethical complexity, though now we must. Such complexity overloads our mental and emotional circuits and overwhelms our capacity to respond, and that causes us to be afraid. We know something about good and evil, but we cannot unravel its intricacies. We see, but we cannot take it all in. The best that we can do in this fallen world is to hone our skills in making responsible ethical decisions. But the central processing units of our moral souls are too slow for the task, like pocket calculators sorting vast spreadsheets. Life as we chose it in the garden simply comes at us too fast. And yet we still remain accountable to conduct life as God has designed it, because we do have access to the "knowledge of good and

49

evil," the moral code of the universe. Our failure is our shame, and our experience is fear.

And so, in the Genesis story when God comes to visit his garden in the cool of that day, Adam and Eve have not only covered themselves, but also hidden themselves in the woods. When God calls out to Adam to ask him where he is, the man responds not only with his whereabouts, but also with his puzzling new condition, "I was naked, and I was afraid." His justification for his separation from God is his own experience of inadequacy, his own shame-fueled fear. After the fall, the thought and action of the humans has become rooted in their own experience of themselves rather than their experience of God and each other. They have become the center of the world they have chosen, taking the place of the forbidden tree in the middle of it all. They have taken on the moral function of God, and so their relationship to God has changed substantively. Created to respond with delight to the voice of their heavenly Father, they now cower in shameful fear whenever he comes around.

In proclaiming God's word, we often present shame as the result of sin. While this is certainly correct, it does not really explain the manner in which shame takes control of our lives. In the garden, the sin of rebellion fosters the experience of shame for the man and his wife, which in turn leads them to sin again by hiding from God. Shame is both the effect and the cause of human sin: we sin, we feel inadequate, then sin again in futile attempts to resolve those feelings. The whole thing is a vicious cycle that consumes the human soul. Those who deal with addiction know this cycle all too well. For instance, in his extensive research on sexual addiction, Patrick Carnes has identified this pattern in the compulsions of his subjects: the addict's emotional life parallels the proverbial roller coaster. If unable to stave off the pain with sex, the addict plunges into despair. When another sexual binge occurs after the addict has promised to stop, the addict despairs again. When she or he has to invent more lies, or if somehow the lies are unmasked, the addict despairs again. Shame drives the sex addict's behavior, and shame is also the reaction to being out of control.[5] This same shame cycle is precisely the theme of Robert Lewis Stevenson's ever relevant *The Strange Case of Dr. Jekyll and Mr. Hyde.*

---

5 Carnes, *Don't Call It Love,* 24.

Some years ago, I ministered for an extended time to a homeless crack addict who had committed his life to Christ and desperately wanted to change his circumstances. The man would go for considerable periods without using the highly addictive drug, but he would always return to it. I would point out that the man had gone long enough to rid his system of the drug and ask him why he thought he always starting using again. The man's response was always the same, "I just feel so terrible about what I have done to my life, and I want to escape!" In a particularly prescient moment, the addict told me, "You know, for twenty years I have been chasing the first crack high I ever had. Now, smoking it only numbs me for a while." Of course, the rewiring of the human brain explains the addict's physiological response, but only the shame cycle explains the spiritual response.

We need not be what society labels "addicts" in order to understand this downward spiral. We are all shame-based sin junkies. The first sin of the garden is essentially a sin of consumption, the eating of fruit from a forbidden tree. Shame's looping message of inadequacy compels us to take for ourselves whatever we think might make us feel and appear adequate. We are ever chasing the thrills of our first purchases, our first sexual encounters, our first days of employment, our first unexposed lies, whatever. These were moments we felt invincible, like gods, if only. For an instant. Our liberty has become the prison of our shame. The problem is ever our shame-driven, soulless consumption. We always drink our shame with a sin chaser. It is like throwing good money after bad, again and again.

We must recognize here that we are engaged in a spiritual battle for the very control of God's creation. The outcome of that war is already determined through the life, death, and resurrection of Jesus Christ, which only makes the enemy all the more desperate to take captive every soul possible before the end comes like a thief in the night. Satan has managed to corrupt this world by drawing humans into his shame trap, disguising it as the true meaning of good life itself.

Most people misunderstand the manner in which Satan traps people through shame, believing their choices to be a simple matter of good and bad. Especially in Western culture, we envision ourselves as independent actors making clear, rational decisions between right and wrong. If it were that easy, no one would ever fall from God's grace. When the trap is baited with poisoned horseradish, the mice do not bite. That is why we bait mousetraps with peanut butter or cheese, things that are generally good and pleasing to little rodents.

When he wants to ambush us, Satan lures us with things that God intended to be good, and then drops the hammer. A mouse is fortunate to find a chunk of salubrious cheese; unless, that is, it sits on a trigger that releases a metal bar to crush its skull. So it is with the bait of Satan, who uses the good things God has created to trap us, by tempting us to misuse them. For example, the sexual expression God created as good to bind the man to his wife and procreate his people, Satan laces with the poison of selfish lust rooted in shame. This is how it always works. The life celebration becomes the debauched party, the call to prevail becomes competitive obsession with success at any cost, the impulse to utilize becomes the insatiable thirst to possess, haute cuisine becomes gluttony, and wisdom becomes pride, and so on. Satan baits us with the merely good and instantly pleasurable to push aside the sacred great and eternally significant.

Righteousness involves fulfilling God's perfect design for his creation, stewarding well all that is his with all that we are. Sin is the misuse and abuse of God's creation, using the right things in the wrong ways. One way leads to holiness and life, the other to shame and death. And Satan is no fool and so does not trap us in blatantly foolish ways. He understands the essence of our desire for the good things God has made, mutating healthy desires that God has given us. When we utilize those things to glorify ourselves rather than God, we move outside of God's will and enshrine ourselves in temples of sin and shame. Satan uses the transactions of this world to bind us to the created order and trap us in time: every swipe of a credit card, touch of a smartphone, and post to Facebook or Instagram, whatever. None of these things is evil in and of itself, but when we overextend to compensate for our sense of inadequacy and cannot separate ourselves, we are every bit as trapped as the cheese-seeking mouse. This is the truth captured by Paul in Romans 3:23 when he writes, "all have sinned and fall short of the glory of God." Simply put, our lives are far less than God created them to be. The only end to this shame cycle apart from God's intervention is death.

While shame reveals our sin and exposes it to the conviction of the Holy Spirit, it also lays the foundation of ongoing sin unless it is resolved. This remains true even if we embrace the forgiveness of the cross. God's forgiveness takes care of his righteous judgment, but it does not change our essential nature of rebellion. The shame of that rebellion perpetuates our pattern of sinfulness, necessitating again and again the efficacy of the cross. Unfortunately, this sin and shame loop has often served the church well. We have mastered the art of presenting a grave crisis requiring a catharsis only the cross (and the church) can provide. Those lost in sin and shame rightly cry out for more. They do not just want to die forgiven people; they want to be out of the shame cycle! They are searching for the re-creation of the resurrection.

Shamelessness in the New Garden —Third Movement

The ultimate power to reverse the downward spiral of sin and shame and create a virtuous cycle of grace and joy is found uniquely in the cross and resurrection of Jesus Christ, together. While these two timeless "events" are often addressed independently, they are actually one single dramatic movement of God to initiate a re-creation of the world. In fact, we should rightly say that this movement continues and will not be completed until the appearance of a "new heaven and new earth" at the end of time as we know it. In the cross/resurrection intervention, God has reversed the flywheel of human history that was accelerating toward death and despair and started it turning again toward life and hope. This is not only the triumph of good over evil in the world, as we are prone to observe, but also the triumph of love over fear in human existence. This is the triumph of which John writes when he declares, "Perfect love drives out fear" (John 1:18).

The burgeoning science of brain research is helping us to understand how God has created us and how the love of Christ has the power to re-create us. Essentially, this relatively new science is showing us that fear and love cannot coexist in the human brain at the same time. Numerous studies using MRI scans have found that fear stimulates the R-complex in our brains, commonly called "the reptilian brain." The reptilian brain is activated subconsciously, so it is hard for us to get at. Often, we may not even know why we are afraid or what we are afraid of, but we feel it in our guts, as it were. This is for our protection, allowing us to react to threats before we even know they are there, but when our fear responses are constantly activated by stress and tension, they go into overdrive. When we cannot get rid of this fear, it becomes anxiety, despair, and depression. Essentially, our fear responses just will not turn off in the morally complex world of sin and shame.

There is one exception: love deactivates the fear response. Using the same fMRI scans, researchers have found that love activates the prefrontal cortex, or conscious brain, and actually shuts down the fear response in the reptilian brain. This is surely an amazing component of God's divine design. The problem is that a stimulus that continually activates our fear response likewise eventually shuts down the love response for which we were created. Our souls are virtual war zones in which fear and love, evil and good, do battle every moment of our natural lives.[6]

One intriguing thing that scientists have discovered recently is that fear and love can initially look a lot alike. Both responses stimulate the release of the hormone oxytocin in the brain in order to deeply imprint specific memories. Both fear and love have the power to embed nearly indelible memories in the brain.[7] You probably know this instinctively. Just think about some terrible experience in your life, and you can feel like you are right back there. When I think of my daughter's emergency surgery fifteen years ago, I still feel like I have just been kicked in the stomach. Now think about someone you really love. Picture their face. Can you feel that, too? When I see my wife, Debbie, or even think about her, a sort of peacefulness

---

6 A useful summary of this research can be found in Eckstein et al., "Oxytocin."

7 One good research article on this phenomenon is Paul, "Love Hormone."

settles into my body that I cannot really explain. When she is with me, I feel less fear.

When these two responses are mixed, it can be really perplexing. When we are afraid of people that we love, our brains cannot figure out how to respond, and we become confused. The switches in our brains just keep firing back and forth until they are worn out. We lose energy. Eventually, we will settle into a fear response, and the love response will be turned off. Fear is powerful because it happens somewhere beneath the surface and cannot be easily unraveled. But it can be turned off by real love.

Perhaps even more intriguing in this vein is recent research published in the journal *Brain and Behavior*. Yale University researchers have found that selfless love—a deep and genuine wish for the happiness of others—actually turns off the brain's reward centers. That is very interesting, because we have known for a long time that falling in love romantically turned those same centers on. One researcher found that a brain newly "in love" looked much like a brain on cocaine. But selfless love, genuine concern for the well-being of others, has the opposite effect.[8] In the language of the Bible, this means that eros (romantic love) and agape (the selfless love of Christ) have very different effects on the brain. Romantic love satisfies reward centers, but selfless love shuts those same centers down. The former causes excitement much like fear, but the latter floods the body with a sense of peace and contentment.

Of course, all truth is God's truth, but we are always amazed when modern science rediscovers truths clearly expounded in the Bible. Today's neuroscience echoes the two-thousand-year-old wisdom of John grounded in the cross and resurrection. "[God] sent his one and only Son into the world that we might live through him," he writes. "The one who fears is not made perfect in love" (1 John 4:9 and 18). He notes that "fear has to do with punishment" (v. 18), which is to say that the human condition of sin and shame entraps a fallen world in a web of fear. But God's love—the forgiveness of the cross and re-creation of the resurrection—changes everything. In the new garden of the resurrection, fear has been driven out! In this new

---

8 Hathaway, "Meditation Helps Pinpoint Neurological Differences."

garden, "we are like Jesus" (v. 17). We are the offspring of the last Adam, the new gardener.

Thus, Paul is able to proclaim of life in the new creation, "There is now no condemnation for those who are in Christ Jesus" (Rom 8:1). In this same declaration, Paul expounds further, "If the Spirit of him who raised Jesus from the dead is living in you, he who raised Christ from the dead will also give life to your mortal bodies because of his Spirit who lives in you" (Rom 8:11). Forgiven in Christ's cross, we are re-created in the resurrection for lives free from shame in the new garden.

Living in the New Garden —Fourth Movement

For the purpose of this conversation, we need to recognize that the Western church has mastered the art of weeding the garden, but often failed to reseed it. Seen in the earlier illustration of nurturing a healthy lawn, the goal of weeding is not to produce bare ground but healthy strands of grass in fertile soil. Similarly, God's plan in the cross/resurrection event is not to produce lives free of sin, but to reproduce lives in his image. If the forgiveness of the cross clears the ground of the soul, then the resurrection is the instrument with which the new gardener replants the Creator's image. The church must revision itself as the "body of Christ"—the body of the new gardener—and thus the tender of fruit-bearing plants, not merely the killer of weeds. In its obsession with the cross, sin, and forgiveness for sin, the church is missing its joyful opportunity to invite those forgiven to "take hold of life that is truly life" (1 Tim 6:19). Though he clearly offered forgiveness and called for repentance, Jesus never claimed that he had come merely so that we could be perpetually forgiven. Rather, he said that he had come so that we "may have life, and have it to the full" (John 10:10). We often miss the word "may" in this statement (Gk *echösin*), a word implying permission being given to lay claim to the abundant life of the new garden. In the local church I pastor, the process of claiming the resurrection and taking hold of this new creation is called whole life discipleship.

If we are right in claiming that the Genesis 3 story of the fall should not be read as a simple morality tale, then neither should the conclusion of that narrative be seen as God's punishment for sin (as it is usually read). We do not think that Genesis 3:14–19 sounds like a condemnatory judgment from the Creator, but rather as a solemn diagnosis of reality after the fall. In this passage, God describes what a world marred by shame will look like and tells Adam and Eve what they have lost as a natural consequence of their decision to misuse the garden.

Our contention is that everything lost in the fall is being restored in the new creation of the resurrection, and that is what we will explore in the remainder of this book. Procreation and parenting are burdens in the fall (Gen 3:16a), but the New Testament offers hope to parents in the new garden. Gender inequality, social hierarchy, and broken marriage are products of the fall (Gen 3:16b), but the New Testament speaks of love, equality, and servanthood in the new garden. Consumerism and hoarding result from the fall (Gen 3:17), but the New Testament tells us that stewardship and generosity are restored in the new garden. The joy of work is lost in the fall (Gen 3:18–19a), but the New Testament tells us that we can find it again in the new garden. Death is the sentence of the fall (Gen 3:19b), but the New Testament proclaims life in new garden.

The fall closed behind us the gate to the garden of Eden, but the opening of Christ's empty tomb is a doorway into the new garden for every whole life disciple of Jesus. Just as he said, Jesus is the new "gate" (Gk *thyra*) by which we are invited to find the "green pasture" of the new garden (John 10:9). It is there if we choose to enter it, and the church may become the harbinger of a new heaven and new earth.

CHAPTER 3:

WORK

So I hated life, because the work that is done under the sun was grievous to me. All of it is meaningless, a chasing after the wind. I hated all the things I had toiled for under the sun, because I must leave them to the one who comes after me. And who knows whether that person will be wise or foolish? Yet they will have control over all the fruit of my toil into which I have poured my effort and skill under the sun. This too is meaningless. So my heart began to despair over all my toilsome labor under the sun. For a person may labor with wisdom, knowledge and skill, and then they must leave all they own to another who has not toiled for it. This too is meaningless and a great misfortune. What do people get for all the toil and anxious striving with which they labor under the sun? All their days their work is grief and pain; even at night their minds do not rest. This too is meaningless. A person can do nothing better than to eat and drink and find satisfaction in their own toil. This too, I see, is from the hand of God, for without him, who can eat or find enjoyment? To the person who pleases him, God gives wisdom, knowledge and happiness, but to the sinner he gives the task of gathering and storing up wealth to hand it over to the one who pleases God. This too is meaningless, a chasing after the wind. (Eccl 2:17–26)

Your work is going to fill a large part of your life, and the only way to be truly satisfied is to do what you believe is great work. And the only way to do great work is to love what you do. If you haven't found it yet, keep looking. Don't settle. As with all matters of the heart, you'll know when you find it.[9]

Human beings are truly remarkable, the crowning glory of God's labor of love in creation. What made humans different from any other creatures on earth? You could point out that we reason and have emotion, even though we now know that some other animals do as well. You might say that we communicate, though just about every other living thing on earth communicates in some way, as well. If you pointed out that we use language, you would be headed in the right direction. But linguists say that the reason we probably use language is that we had something we needed to talk about, and that would be the exchange of goods and services. We are the only creatures that are actually working, intentionally producing something of value to others than ourselves, and that makes us very unique indeed. God designed and created us to work, to do something useful. And work is a huge part of our lives. We laugh when we hear people talk about "work-life balance," surely one of the most

---

9 Jobs, *BrainyQuote.*

overused catchphrases of our compartmentalized culture, a phrase we employ in our endless search for some sort of guilt-free equilibrium. We always follow with a question, "Is work something other than your life?" What we usually mean, really, is that we might be identifying ourselves too exclusively by our work, failing to recognize that we are much more than what we do. But what we find helpful is to realize that we only have one life and all of our relationships and interactions comprise it, including our work.

The problem is that we have lost our perspective on work and forgotten that we were designed to work passionately, and we can trace that problem back directly to original sin. Understand we are not just speaking of an income-producing job or career here, but about all of the work that we do, from yard work to mission work. In Christ's resurrection and the re-creation that it has ushered in, we have been restored as the tillers of God's garden, the new Eden.

Work in the First Garden
—First Movement

One of the reasons the Bible is easy to relate to and remains the number one bestseller is that many of the various images to depict God are drawn from human life. We see God in his social roles as a father, teacher, and king, and in his personal relationships he is a friend and lover. There is yet another image type and that is the portraying of God in his role as a worker. Robert Banks has captured a number of different human work images in the Bible that relate to God: composer and performer; metalworker and potter; garment maker and dresser; gardener and orchardist; farmer and wine grower; shepherd and pastoralist; tentmaker and camper; builder and architect. The spirit of God tells us about the character of God in such images. As we are in the image of God, these images display the variety, beauty, and diversity of work that apply to us. Of course, God is much more, as the apostle Paul said now we see dimly, but he is the perfect worker, father, friend, and teacher. Banks goes on, "the coming of Christ resulted not in the end of these images, but in their fulfillment and resurrection. What we witness as a result of the incarnation is nothing less than a genuine re-creation of the human imagination as part of the creation of a new humanity in Christ."[10]

So often in Christian circles, we hear people talk of God, especially God the Father, under the umbrella of all the various "Omni's," omnipresent and the like. Helpful as that is, it is important to take hold of the fact that the Bible gives a much more tangible and readable face to God in the images drawn from our own human experience. It is good theology to focus on these images as well.

So when we speak of work in the garden, what was it like and meant to be, we have all the rich imagery of God the worker throughout Scripture to guide us. Work in the garden was a place for the potter, the shepherd, and the builder, for practical, creative, and entrepreneurial giftedness. Let us just reflect on two of the socioeconomic images of biblical times for a moment—potter and shepherd. Arts and crafts are very much in vogue

---

10 Banks, *God the Worker*, 12.

today. We love the creativity expressed in clay kitchenware or the imagination displayed in a needlework piece that pictures village life. In biblical times, so much of value was dependent upon the potter's wheel. It is a trade we still understand today. God in his work is a potter. He is a craftsman: "the earth takes shape like clay under a seal; its features stand out like those of a garment" (Job 38:14). We respond to the beauty of his work with awe and wonder. When one walks the Appalachian trail or stands at the foot of Uluru, there is the experience of connecting to sacred spaces, and holy ground. The Divine Potter is our lover who shapes us and molds to his perfect purposes. The prophet Isaiah reminds us, "Yet you, LORD, are our Father. We are the clay, you are the potter; we are all the work of your hand" (Isa 64:8).

In our own work, whether it be our volunteering, ministry at church, or our paid employment, does not the image of the Divine Potter speak to us? We look for times of creativity, of doing something special, of showing love and care. The assembly line is dark and restrictive, but it does not define our life and "work" experiences.

The image of shepherd was commonly used for ancient Near Eastern kings and in the Father, and in Jesus, we have the ultimate good shepherd. The prophets speak of good shepherding as healing, nurturing, fair, and overseeing, with the sheep's best interests at heart (Ezek 34:4). As Jesus declared, the good shepherd models sacrifice: "Very truly I tell you Pharisees, anyone who does not enter the sheep pen by the gate, but climbs in by some other way, is a thief and a robber" (John 10:1). The risen Christ exhorts his disciples to look after his sheep (John 21:16) and elders are to act as shepherds over the flock (Acts 20:28). The live metaphor of God the good shepherd inspires the worker to be a healing agent, one who nurtures even the "lost," and to put others before one's own selfish pursuits or ambition. It speaks to the employer and the employee alike. We are in his image, so reflecting on all of these images assists us not only in our comprehension of God, but of the expansive nature of work.

When we read Genesis 1–2, it is evident God enjoys his work, particularly in creating a cosmic garden. God looked out over all of his labor and it was good (Gen 1:31). These garden chapters are very much about work; three times in Genesis 2–3 alone, we are told that God had been at work. It is part of who God is, and it is part of being authentically human.

Now work is wider than having a job. Banks and Preece explain, "work can potentially include all sorts of effort and activity. About the only activities we would generally not describe as work are sleeping and eating (except a business lunch!), engaging in hobbies and playing sports (except professionally), watching TV or a movie, going to church or a concert."[11] Also, work is made for humanity, not humanity for work, so work that is meaningful and authentic should reflect the character of God the worker.

The garden picture is so different from the other understanding of work in biblical times. The Greek elite thought ordinary work was only for the uneducated, the slave. It was the creative work, the philosopher's task or the ruler that was admired. In the Mesopotamian accounts, "human beings work to supply food for the selfish, lazy gods."[12] In God's garden humans are honored and empowered and as image bearers are

---

11 Banks and Preece, *Getting the Job Done Right,* 13.

12 Matthews, *Genesis 1–11:26,* 209.

caretakers for all of God's handiwork. As we say in the chapter on stewardship, this would mean managing and developing all of God's resources to promote well-being for all. Humankind is to work the garden and take care of it (Gen 2:15). The word translated work here is the one commonly used in the Old Testament for tilling the soil, service to others, labor, and worship. In this work humanity is to exercise godly stewardship and the words "subdue" and "ruled" indicated the immense trust God had in humanity in their "work" (Gen 1:26–28).

The imagery of God the worker reveals the richness of work and the image embraces so many areas of life, whether we are retired or off to school.

Work Lost
—Second Movement

The fall describes how the joy of work has been flattened by drudgery. Resources like the ground, which were humanity's servant, are now seen as toxic. The imagery is vivid. Orchards are overrun by thistles, and productive, meaningful labor is now known for its hardship, drudgery, bitterness, and sweat. Tragically, for some, lack of meaningful work will lead to loss of self-esteem and mental health issues. Australian Catholic University Professor Jim Bright states, "The fear, anxiety, social exclusion and depression that can accompany unemployment are well documented. Unemployment and under-employment are well established as being injurious to our health. Despite this, we persist in demonising work . . . work, if not seen as a cause of depression, certainly exacerbates the condition."[13]

It can all appear meaningless as to dirt we return. God has spoken and his chastisement is that the agricultural ground, the focus of early humanity's work, is cursed. The verses read:

> Cursed is the ground because of you; through painful toil you will eat food from it all the days of your life. It will produce thorns and thistles for you, and you will eat the plants of the field. By the sweat of your brow you will eat your food until you return to the ground, since from it you were taken; for dust you are and to dust you will return. (Gen 3:17b–19)

---

13 Bright, *Telling Your Employer*, 9.

Dramatically Adam and Eve are expelled from the garden. Literally, they are banished. The garden was the foundation from which humanity was to spread the blessings of Eden to all the earth. Now that foundation is lost (Gen 3:23). Angels are placed at the east end of the garden to keep humanity out. They no longer even return to care for the garden as the Hebrew word for guard also implies that the angels are now the carers. Now as Adam and Eve no longer cultivate God's garden they must find and work their own plot of land.

The result will be that humanity becomes dominated by work, which will become a god in itself. It will even define us as honor is given to those who get the most "land" (i.e. the best jobs). Yet work is seen as a curse with our use of a plethora of terms such as burnout, work stress, and living for the weekend.

Scripturally, it is hard to contemplate a sadder fate for fallen humanity. In music, we sing along with "I don't like Mondays" and we eat at "Thank God It's Fridays"!

Work in the New Garden
—Third Movement

Is all lost? Is all work overwhelmed by the "curse"? Can the redeeming power of the risen Christ re-imagine work? Jacques Ellul in his penetrating critique is pessimistic, born from his understanding of the depth of the fall on God's structures of creation, as well as the dehumanizing nature of much of today's institutional and technological work settings. The world of bureaucracies and IT is not a relational, love of neighbor one. He states,

> I am in a society which organizes work in a coercive and totalitarian way, in a system of professions which is absurd or unjust, in atomized work, in an economic order which I cannot accept. I live to work. The more society organizes itself, the more it thrusts the totality of my life in this work, so that I have to try as much as I can to keep the main thread of life clear of entanglement.[14]

---

14 Ellul, *Ethics of Freedom*, 436–37.

Nicholas Wolterstorff is more open to a positive social transformation with respect to work that is inspired by the motif of the resurrection (1 Cor 15:58). He states, "Can we *entirely* alter what we do, so that here and now we practice the occupations of heaven? Of course not. Can we *somewhat* alter what we do, so that our occupations come closer to becoming our God-issued vocation? Usually, yes."[15] And many who enjoy and receive fulfillment from their work would readily agree with Wolterstorff. But that is not everyone's world.

Let us turn to the Reformation because in that revolution some helpful developments were birthed with respect to work. The Reformation, to the surprise of many, was more than a justification by faith movement!

Prior to the sixteenth century Reformation there was a tendency, still seen today in some Christian circles, to restrict a vocation or calling to "spiritual" roles. Only the minister or missionary is called. The Reformers spoke more of vocation in a broad sense, a calling from the Lord in all areas of service that

---

15 Wolterstorff, "More on Vocation," 20–23.

fulfills the first garden mandate to rule and subdue the world for God's glory. Martin Luther's view of vocation and calling encompassed all three "traditional stations of life: household, economy, state and church."[16]

This was an empowering transformation with respect to work as all work, not just pastoral ministry roles, are God-given callings and vocations. The handyman, teacher, and house parent are called. Yet, in all of this Luther still had a strong sense of the fall, as well as the tension of living and working in a society where the kingdom and resurrection life was still awaited in its fullness.

Luther's society was also not one of great mobility, especially as far as vocation was concerned. Today we take it for granted that we are global citizens work wise, and regular job changing is a frequent happening for most. For social stability, verses like 1 Corinthians 7:20 were pivotal for Luther's world: "Each man must remain in that condition in which he was called" (1 Cor 7:20).

---

16 Althaus, *Ethics of Martin Luther,* 36.

There was more flexibility in Calvin's approach to vocation and his vision of a "Christ transforming culture," and our union with Christ would encourage a more optimistic, joyful approach to the totality of vocation. Yet in the Reformers' day, there was not a job vacancy section in the local paper and choices were few! The Puritans, likewise, understandably took a conservative stance about change:

> [This] no doubt had the same roots as it did for Luther and Calvin: a strong doctrine of Providence; the 1 Corinthians 7 command to remain in one's calling; a desire to spare Christians the restlessness and lure of ambition and greed linked with job-hopping; and a still quite static, rigidly structured society all around them, in which a "situation vacant" was rare . . . there were virtually no schools . . . which have created the totally new situation whereby most people are equipped for a variety of jobs and there is now such a thing as a choice of work.[17]

---

17 Hart, "The Teachings of the Puritans," 199.

In our mobile age the Reformers' understanding of work through the lens of vocation needs re-imagining. We thank God for the vocation revolution the Reformation instigated but a new God-given prophetic word is needed.

The popular theologian Miroslav Volf looks to the dehumanizing nature of much global work, its spirit of alienation, to direct our thoughts to a charismatic theology of work—gifts. The ministry of the Spirit of the risen Christ is not confined to the church, nor for Volf are spiritual gifts. And by gifts one is not just speaking of the extraordinary gifts like tongues, but ordinary work like helps and administration. The biblical listing of gifts (e.g. 1 Cor 12) is not a fixed one, so a re-imagined list of gifts is appropriate, that considers our mobile, multitasking age. Gifts like economic management, vision, entrepreneurship, and general management enhance that biblical list. And gifts envisage a dual partnership—humanity and God working together for a better world.

This working together would ensure a balance between the pursuit of excellence in all that we do and a spirit of humbleness. Paul in 1 Corinthians 12–14, in his general instruction on gifts, is aware the church is striving after abilities and empowerments. He does not pour a bucket of water over the striving but warns against giftedness or leadership having as its foundation boastfulness or selfishness. Gifts are for building up the church, or in Volf's context, the broader community as well (1 Cor 14:12).

The key for Paul is 1 Corinthians 13. This chapter is strategically placed between two specific chapters on gifts—12 and 14. It is an arch over the chapters that centers on love and it reminds us that gifts and vocation are not an end in themselves. They are part of our life calling us to love God and love our neighbor as ourselves. They are a means to serving and fulfilling that end. The use of gifts or vocation for selfish ambition, self-aggrandisement or a puffed-up view of excellence are an anathema for Paul. It is about love! This great love chapter is tragically often divorced from its primary context—gifts. Paul declares:

> Love is patient, love is kind and is not jealous;
> love does not brag and is not arrogant, does not
> act unbecomingly; it does not seek its own, is not

provoked, does not take into account a wrong suffered, does not rejoice in unrighteousness, but rejoices with the truth; bears all things, believes all things, hopes all things, endures all things . . . But now faith, hope, love, abide these three; but the greatest of these is love. (1 Cor 13:4–13 NASB)

With the spirit of agape, we follow our vocation, calling in all areas of life and ministry. Jesus's lordship demands nothing less. Jesus had a background as a tradesman (Matt 13:55) and his parables reveal he was intimately aware of the workers' world (e.g. Luke 13:6–9). Whilst we are not given much detail on his specific views on work, his teaching, like the Sermon on the Mount, challenges most of our basic assumptions about life, including work. The Beatitudes call us to care for the powerless and the sermon instructs us to walk the talk, and to live out the values of the kingdom (Matt 5–8). Jesus exhorted:

No good tree bears bad fruit, nor does a bad tree bear good fruit. Each tree is recognized by its own fruit. People do not pick figs from thornbushes, or grapes from briers. A good man

84

brings good things out of the good stored up in his heart, and an evil man brings evil things out of the evil stored up in his heart. For the mouth speaks what the heart is full of. (Luke 6:43–45)

In the risen Christ our days are transformed!

Living in the New Garden —Fourth Movement

A senior judge recently shared with me that he sincerely believed that apart from his legal expertise and experience he had received the gift of wisdom for the serious cases he had to decide. He shared that he had a particularly difficult case where he could not find a fair way forward. In prayer, he asked the risen Lord to continue to guide and direct his path, and to bestow upon him the wisdom he especially needed at this time. Overnight the answer came to him and he had a strong conviction that the judgment he gave was a result of God's grace working on the natural talents he had bestowed on him. His vocation, being a judge, was at its best when he worked in partnership with the

Lord's gifts, seeking to love God and those he brought before him as judge.

The re-imagining of garden work through the lens of the resurrection calls us to apply the best insights from creation, vocation, and gifts to reshape our everyday work. Realistically, work immersed in the complexity of technological optimism, unemployment growth, and job "worship" will not be fully redeemed and restored until the return of Christ. Romans 8:19–22 promises the restoration of all-natural creation processes. However, as Wolterstorff says, that does not mean we cannot constructively alter now what we do. We should fight for God-honoring work practices across all cultures that restore the joy of the garden and that take us back across the threshold of that banished utopia. What is the purpose of kingdom living if it does not lead to community transformation in employment standards, leadership values, the assembly line, and the ensuring of meaningful work for all?

In our work we do it all in the name of the risen Christ, giving thanks to the Father through him. We believe all work is valuable, equal, and God-given, whatever our role and calling.

This is the priesthood of all believers. We are the image of God the worker! We are about the Father's business. We seek work practices that are ethical. We look for ways of service that help others and allow the community to flourish. We take action on unjust practices and advocate for those who are committed to a fair wage, environmentally friendly practices, and good working conditions. We oppose sweatshops.[18]

---

18 For example, see Transform Australia Advocacy for fair work practices in the global fashion industry (NSW Baptist Aid website).

CHAPTER 4:

WHOLENESS
AND WELLNESS

---

*Whatever you do, whether in word or deed, do it
all in the name of the Lord Jesus, giving thanks
to God the Father through him. (Col 3:17 NIV)*

*And if Christ has not been raised, our preaching
is useless and so is your faith. More than that,
we are then found to be false witnesses about
God, for we have testified about God that he
raised Christ from the dead. But he did not
raise him if in fact the dead are not raised. For*

if the dead are not raised, then Christ has not been raised either. And if Christ has not been raised, your faith is futile; you are still in your sins. Then those also who have fallen asleep in Christ are lost. If only for this life we have hope in Christ, we are of all people most to be pitied. But Christ has indeed been raised from the dead, the firstfruits of those who have fallen asleep. (1 Cor 15:14–20 NIV)

I am tired of chanting in languages which are not my own, yet I can't make sense of the world, can't reconcile human suffering with a compassionate God, unless I incorporate a philosophy of reincarnation. I love the rich earthiness of the Goddess religions. I love the way they speak directly to my female experience of the world, the way they honour life and fertility, change and growth. Yet all logic in me riles at the notion of a deity of either gender: I am attracted to the figure of Jesus—to his compassion, his courage, his fear, his humanity, the way he is born and dies, journeys through

89

*the underworld and lives again, like the great
heroes of mythology. Yet Christianity requires a
leap of faith of such magnitude that I feel I must
parcel up all reason and leave it on the far side
of some rocky gorge. So I choose not to throw in
my lot with any single theology. I practise yoga,
read Christian and Buddhist texts with equal
interest and pray to a God who is no less real
for its diverse husbandry.*[19]

MindBodySpirit festivals, or their like, are a global phenomenon. They are a place for people to explore spirituality, especially those who see themselves as "spiritual, but not religious," or as one of the growing number of the "Nones" (no affiliation with any specific religious group). For many years, I have had a booth in a MindBodySpirit festival in Sydney and have co-founded the Community of Hope that reaches out to those exploring such spirituality.

Those drawn to these alternative religious movements, "New Spirituality," tend to have a desire for a spirituality that

19 Trenoweth, *Future of God*, x–xi.

is eclectic and that emphasizes "self-spirituality." The term "eclectic" points to a drawing on a range of resources from Buddhism, Tarot, Mind Powers to Christianity. The expression "self-spirituality" indicates that this seeker is committed to personal transformation, to be the best person they can possibly be. It is about the finding and achieving of "wellness." Elizabeth Gilbert in her globally successful book *Eat, Pray, Love* typifies this search:

> Flexibility is just as essential for divinity as is discipline. Your job, then, should you choose to accept it, is to keep searching for the metaphors, rituals and teachers that will help you move ever closer to divinity. The Yogic scripture say that God responds to the sacred prayers and the efforts of human beings in any way whatsoever that mortals choose to worship—just so long as those prayers are sincere. As one line from the Upanishads suggests: People follow different paths, straight or crooked, according to their temperament, depending on which they consider

best or most appropriate—and all reach You,

just as rivers enter the ocean.[20]

The extraordinary truth is that many seeking "wellness" through such spiritualities today are often, by their beliefs, not advocating wholeness. A MindBodySpirit festival can appear to be committed to a wholistic way of life with an emphasis on concerns such as diet, creation care, animal wellbeing, and yoga but at its heart, there is often a basic denial of wholeness. Let us illustrate. Reincarnation is a popular belief for New Spirituality devotees, yet it ultimately denies the material—our physical bodies. It speaks of a world where one's spirit/soul escapes the body to migrate into another body. Ultimately, our current bodies do not count, especially for eternity. Compare this to the Judeo-Christian belief in the resurrection of the body. In this worldview, the whole of me counts to God; all of me goes to be with him for eternity. That is a gospel of "wellness"— wholeness! Tragically many Christians do not appreciate or know of the resurrection of the body and by such ignorance fail to grip the wholeness of resurrection living.

---

20 Gilbert, *Eat, Pray, Love,* 206.

Wholeness in the First Garden —First Movement

In chapter 3, we addressed the biblical image of God the worker. In Genesis, we have a picture of God the artisan, the master craftsman who sculpts the pinnacle of his creation. His material is "dust." Loose granular dirt of the ground, rather than clay; almost the contemporary sculptures in the sand. This is also what we return to when we die (Dan 12:2). Poignantly humanity is God's Mona Lisa, his climatic work of art.

Dramatically Genesis depicts Adam and Eve being created as whole people. Old Testament scholar Derek Kidner puts it this way: "that man neither 'has' a soul nor 'has' a body, although for convenience he may be analysed into two or more constituents. The basic truth here: he is a unity."[21] Hebrew thought does not envision a life lived apart from the body. Job cries out, "And after my skin has been destroyed, yet in my flesh I will see God" (Job 19:26).

---

21 Kidner, *Genesis*, 61.

93

Although Adam and Eve are the pinnacle of God's creation there is an overwhelming narrative of dependence. Life is dependent on the Creator, and only occurs because there is a potter. Certainly, it is a creation of immense promise, given vast stewardship responsibility, but its frailty outside of the Creator's hand is evident, nevertheless. The Divine Potter then gives his pride and joy a lasting "kiss," a face-to-face animation of life. Then, "The LORD God formed a man from the dust of the ground and breathed into his nostrils the breath of life, and the man became a living being" (Gen 2:7).

Now the phrase "breath of life" is not the one used elsewhere in the Old Testament for "spirit/wind" (*ruach*), rather it demonstrates the unique and intimate connection between the Creator and creature. "Breath of life" is also possessed by animals (Gen 7:22). But it's humanity alone that God "kisses," and as a consequence the statute of dust majestically transforms into a living being.

Scholar C. John Collins points out that other Mesopotamian accounts from this period say that "man" was made from clay touched with a divine element (e.g. god's spittle), but what is truly unique in Genesis is the relational component. In these other accounts, the gods made humanity to be their workhorses. In Genesis, God does not depend "on his creatures for sustenance," rather his promise for them is "that of enjoyment" and "blessing."[22] The most significant person in the universe creates us for his enjoyment and our wellbeing in all aspects of life.

It is popular in Christian circles today to compare Greek to Hebrew thought. In later Platonic thought salvation for the soul meant liberation from the body, a little like today's "New Spirituality." The immaterial soul (psyche) was immortal and was the core of humanity that really counted. Contrast this with the wholeness of the living person in Genesis 1–2. Kenneth A. Matthews concludes, "Hebrew thought does not envision life apart from the body (Job 19:26–27). The breath of God assures Adam has life, its absence means death" (e.g. Job 34:14; Ps 104:29).[23] In the biblical worldview, Adam and Eve stand before their maker as a model of wholeness.

---

22 Collins, Genesis 1–4, 241.

23 Matthews, *Genesis 1–11:26*, 199.

Wholeness Lost
—Second Movement

Dictionaries define "wholeness" as "a thing complete in itself," "in a single unit not broken into parts." Healthy living, wellness, is knowing we are complete in ourselves and that all parts of us count to God. God is not just concerned about one part of me, say my "soul," but with all of me. Throughout this book, our chapters address what it means to practice wholeness in work, rest, marriage, and stewardship. They are the components of a sound, balanced, and healthy life. These components, as we see in this book, have been seriously "messed up" in the fall and we live life as fractured people. Unfortunately, at times, we give up on material wellbeing and settling for a spiritual salvation in the world to come.

This wholeness/wellness breakdown is poignantly illustrated in the early chapters of Genesis. Adam and Eve leave the garden as homeless people. Kicked out they become "wanderers" in search of a home. The relationship between Cain and Abel is immediately fractured and, as Genesis 3 portrays,

96

all of life is becoming toilsome and difficult. In the tower of Babel account in Genesis 11, there is a pathetic attempt to unify humanity in a new city with a landmark tower, made of makeshift materials, brick, and tar instead of stone and mortar (Gen 11:3). It is all futile. The crumbling city results in further fragmentation of the people and even the loss of a common language. It is such a contrasting picture to the wellness found in Genesis 1 and 2, of God's love and provision for all aspects of Adam and Eve's life. However, there is still a glimmer of hope that wholeness will be restored. Harvard University's Jewish scholar, Jon Levenson, concludes: "Abraham, Isaac and Jacob continue to exist after they have died, not, it should be underscored, as disembodied spirits but as the people whose fathers they will always be. That death represents an absolute terminus, as it does to the modern mind, is not a foregone conclusion in biblical thought."[24]

The fall hurts everything, including the sense of being "whole" people who God cares for and who live as "whole" people in his presence. Life becomes compartmentalized, parts

---

24 Levenson, *Resurrection and the Restoration of Israel*, 229.

of which are lived better than others. We can find solace in spiritual things but neglect the truth that eternity is all of me being restored and valued.

Wholeness in the New Garden —Third Movement

The physical resurrection of Jesus is a triumphant declaration of wholeness/wellness for humanity. The fractured nature of being and life that is ours in Adam, resulting from the fall, is reversed. Paul states that the resurrected Jesus can be seen as the firstfruits of the resurrection harvest (1 Cor 15:20). When the farmer tastes the firstfruits of his harvest he experiences a taste sensation, a sample of what is to follow—will this be quality produce? Jesus sets the standard for what is to come. He comes first and then when the end of time comes the dead in Christ will be raised like Christ as whole persons. Let us hear how the apostle Paul explains it:

> But Christ has indeed been raised from the dead, the firstfruits of those who have fallen asleep. For since death came through a man,

the resurrection of the dead comes also through a man. For as in Adam all die, so in Christ all will be made alive. But each in turn: Christ, the firstfruits; then, when he comes, those who belong to him. (1 Cor 15:20–23 NIV)

The resurrection of Jesus clearly demonstrates that God cares for the whole of me so much that he is raising up the whole of me for eternity. This is a revolutionary thought for those who have been taught to believe that the body does not matter and all that counts is the eternal existence of my soul or spirit. If God cares for the whole of me for eternity, obviously he cares for the whole of me now! This is evidenced in the way Jesus cared for people in every aspect of their life. He healed physically, drove out demons, fed the hungry and taught life-changing values. Jesus spent "quality" time with those the elite of his day despised.

This whole person status applies to all people and is to be lived out by the resurrection community. This is revolutionary as in biblical times it was the elite alone who were favored and had status. Paul is inspirational as he teaches:

> Since, then, you have been raised with Christ, set your hearts on things above, where Christ is, seated at the right hand of God. (Col 3:1 NIV) [You] have put on the new self, which is being renewed in knowledge in the image of its Creator. Here there is no Gentile or Jew, circumcised or uncircumcised, barbarian, Scythian, slave or free, but Christ is all, and is in all. (Col 3:10–11 NIV)

Recently I spoke at a service for children, and their parents, who were beginning their studies at high school. It is a strong Christian school. Many present were "fellow travelers," at best, when it came to being followers of Jesus. In a talk on "resurrection values that guide us," I said that around the auditorium walls were plaques listing the brightest students and those who had excelled in sports. And this was good. However, parents should gauge whether this is a school committed to Christian values, by its care for the whole student, irrespective of sporting or academic prowess. Is every student, teacher, staff member in the school treated equally as whole people? What about the most vulnerable student? Some friends later told me that a non-Christian couple who had a disabled son had attended the commencement service. What was said touched their hearts, and if that is what Christianity was about, they were now very open to the same.

In a "spiritual" audit of your place of work, extended family, and neighborhood, ask the question, "Is resurrection wholeness at play?" Caught up in this is Jesus's tag phrase, "Love your neighbor as yourself." It is the foundation for wellness, irrespective of gender, race or economic status (Gal 3:18). These three forms of discrimination in Paul's day remain with us. The world never changes!

As we have seen in the resurrection, there is no status, and the first-century Greek, Roman or Jewish citizen had never witnessed such a world. This is absolutely revolutionary, and it calls for the human dignity and the human worth of all people. In a practical and spiritual way, God births this new reality, by pouring the gift of the Holy Spirit on all people, not just the elite. To be part of the family of God is to stand for one inclusive community, free of all discrimination and racism.

Martin Luther King Jr. expressed this so vividly in his "I Have a Dream" speech, which captured all of our hearts: "I have a dream that my four little children will one day live in a nation where they will not be judged by the color of their skin but by the content of their character. . . . I have a dream today . . . I have a dream that one day every valley shall be exalted, every hill and mountain shall be made low, the rough places will be made plain, and the crooked places will be made straight, and the glory of the Lord shall be revealed and all flesh shall see it together." When the resurrection worldview (dream) is lived out, there is no equal.

Although this message of wholeness in the resurrection of Jesus is good news, that does not mean everyone will initially comprehend it or receive the truth of it gladly. It may offend their worldview. This rejection of the message of wholeness happened for the apostle Paul. In Acts 17, verses 16 to 32, we read that Paul is in Athens, which was a city full of idols. There were many contrasting worldviews. He concluded his brilliant oratory before the Greeks with this theological statement:

"For he has set a day when he will judge the
world with justice by the man he has appointed.
He has given proof of this to everyone by raising
him from the dead." When they heard about the
resurrection of the dead, some of them sneered,
but others said, "We want to hear you again on
this subject." (Acts 17:31–32 NIV)

Why did some scoff? The Greeks in their myths had stories of
a deity coming back from the dead, even if it was not in any
historical sense. But humanity rising as whole people, surely not!
As we have discussed, death for most Greeks meant liberation
of the soul from the body. What was this archaic, uninformed
teaching on the resurrection of the dead? Some were open, and
others moved on. Not all people today will greet the message of
wholeness with glee. Some will seek to find wellness without
it. However, wholeness alone does justice to the significance
of mind, body, and spirit. We are no longer "wanderers" in
search of a home. In Jesus, we have entered God's rest and have
returned to his magnificent garden.

Living in the New Garden —Fourth Movement

Wellness is related to how we view others and ourselves. We are to "walk tall," seeing in the resurrection of Jesus that we were destined to be in the image of the resurrected Christ, now and for eternity—whole people cared for by the Trinity. Whether it be our work, family relationships, friendships, study or play, we are to live out this reality for the wellbeing of others and ourselves. And this truth drives us as we care for the poor and powerless. One "whole" life can make a difference!

We find it helpful when wholeness is a clear focus of our prayer life for others and ourselves. God cares and is concerned for all our experiences in the roller coaster of life. They are petitions for prayer. Wholeness also challenges our diet, physical fitness, and lifestyle. We should look after our whole body. Ironically today, the wholeness/wellness movement has missed or neglected the empowering resurrection focus.

Throughout this book, a key principle is that the resurrection of Jesus restores everything. Not only are we as

104

humans restored as whole people, called to view and treat others with the same love and human dignity, but this restoration also applies to creation. Resurrection living is a taste of what is to come—perfect redemption of the garden in all aspects. Wellness is walking in that light now. Tim Foster has helpfully charted this understanding of the good news of Jesus.[25]

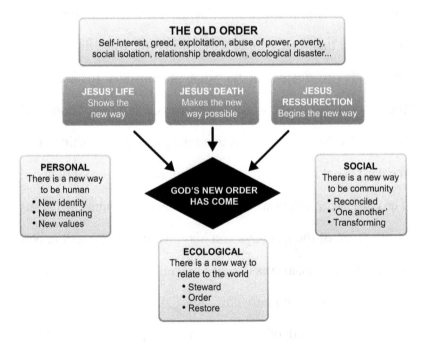

25 Foster, *Suburban Captivity of the Church*, 25.

This truth of personal wholeness is found in an unexpected place. The tarot card pack is the preferred tool for guidance for many today. Its symbols are largely Christian, and it was probably a "PowerPoint presentation" in Renaissance Italy. It was later taken over for occult prediction. During a MindBodySpirit festival, we have numerous conversations with seekers about the cards and the judgment card is of particular importance. It portrays the archangel blowing the trumpet at the end of time and people joyously rising from their graves physically resurrected. On the pennant connected to the angel's trumpet is a red cross, which is a universal symbol of hope and healing. In the conversations that take place it is explained that the card is not one of reincarnation, but resurrection wholeness! The card is consistent with Paul's message in Athens, that Jesus is the judge of the last days and his reward is resurrection. Not all in the festivals, as was the case in Paul's day, respond warmly to the message—but many do!

Does the truth of wholeness stop us speaking of humanity having a soul or spirit? Not at all. The concept of the immortality of the soul was developed in ancient Greek thought and is found

106

in the writings of philosophers such as Plato. The Scriptures never use the expression immortality of the soul as such. As we have seen, the central message of the Bible is that our future is as resurrected people, and even this is dependent on God's grace and Jesus's return. Of course, our physical body is transformed and it is no longer subject to carnal desires and is truly spiritual— the temple of the Holy Spirit (1 Cor 15:42–55). Yet it is no less real and physical than Jesus's resurrection body. Paul declares, "And just as we have borne the image of the earthly man, so shall we bear the image of the heavenly man" (1 Cor 15:49). Eugene Peterson reflecting on Philippians 3:21 says it so well.

> But there's far more to life for us. We're citizens of high heaven! We're waiting the arrival of the Savior, the Master, Jesus Christ, who will transform our earthly bodies into glorious bodies like his own. He'll make us beautiful and whole with the same powerful skill by which he is putting everything as it should be, under and around him. (Phil 3:21 MSG)

Yet even though we are whole people, this does not reject the notion that humans have a material as well as an immaterial

107

aspect to our being. This is part of the wonder and mystery of being human. And it appears that at death this immaterial side of us—soul or spirit—exits as we await the final resurrection. Theologians have called this the "intermediate state." Some feel at this time we may be in "soul sleep," others that we may be clothed with a temporary resurrection body, and yet others that God is beyond time and that we actually die and awake into the day of judgment and resurrection. These are discussions for another day as the focus of the first garden and the new garden is resurrection wholeness. That is how we are to understand ourselves and live: in unity of body and soul, and as a temple of the Holy Spirit. Theologian Mike Bird concludes, "the normal state of human existence is a materialised unity of body and soul. This unity is broken down at death, the immaterial element is preserved in the intermediate state, but body and soul are then reunified at the resurrection."[26]

It is about living now with the promise of wellness and wholeness but knowing that there is a more startling and

---

26 Bird, Evangelical Theology, 665.

complete day awaiting us. This is a vision that drives us.

Wellness living is the tension of "now" but "not yet"! This is

amazingly depicted by Joni Eareckson Tada:

> I can scarcely believe it. I with shrivelled, bent
> fingers, atrophied muscles, gnarled knees, and
> no feeling from the shoulders down, will one
> day have a new body, light, bright, and clothed
> in righteousness—powerful and dazzling. Can
> you imagine the hope this gives someone spinal
> cord-injured like me? Or someone who is cerebral
> palsied, brain-injured, or who has multiple
> sclerosis? Imagine the hope this gives someone
> who is manic depressive. No other religion, no
> other philosophy promises new bodies, hearts
> and minds. Only in the Gospel of Christ do
> hurting people find such incredible hope.[27]

---

27 Eareckson Tada, *Heaven: Your Real Home*, 53.

CHAPTER 5:

LOVE AND MARRIAGE

Have we not all one Father? Has not one God created us? Why then are we faithless to one another, profaning the covenant of our fathers? . . . And this second thing you do. You cover the Lord's altar with tears, with weeping and groaning because he no longer regards the offering or accepts it with favor from your hand. But you say, "Why does he not?" Because the Lord was witness between you and the wife of your youth, to whom you have been faithless, though she is your companion and your wife by covenant. Did he not make them one, with a portion of the Spirit in their union? (Mal 2:10, 13–15a ESV)

They say all marriages are made in heaven, but so are thunder and lightning. ~ Clint Eastwood

Perhaps no topic so dominates Christian discourse and debate today than that surrounding marriage. Not unlike the broader population, followers of Jesus seem to be at a loss to know where to begin when defining what marriage is. Is it a social or legal contract? Is it a basic human right? Is it simply an exclusive relationship between two committed people? Is marriage for the benefit of those in the relationship, does it exist for the good of society, or is its purpose to honor God? There does not even seem to be broad agreement about the right questions to ask. Our premise is that God created marriage both for his glory and for the welfare of his creation. We believe that God's design for marriage was corrupted in the fall and restored in the resurrection.

Whatever marriage is, it is certainly a complex relationship in society today. In the United States, where I reside in the nation's capital, research shows that 40 to 50 percent of all first marriages will end in divorce.[28] In Sydney, Australia, where Ross resides, that number is slightly lower, though still alarmingly high at 38 percent.[29] Not surprisingly, subsequent marriages fare even worse. Suffice it to say that marriage is no simple undertaking throughout the world today.

The good news is that marriage is a far more successful endeavor for those actively involved in the life of a church. Researcher Bradley Wright has found that those Americans who self-identify as Christians are just as likely to have experienced divorce as the general population, around 60 percent. However, he has discovered that among those couples attending church regularly, only 38 percent have been divorced.[30] Similarly, prominent American marriage researcher W. Bradford Wilcox has demonstrated through his analysis of polling that Christians who attend church several times a month or more are 35 percent less likely to divorce than those unaffiliated with local

---

28 United States Census Bureau, 2014.

29 Australian Government, Department of Social Services, 2014.

30 Wright, "Christians Are Hate-Filled Hypocrites," 133.

congregations.[31] Of course, there are all sorts of social factors that might produce such disparities, but could these also be signs of the new gardener's work? We believe that they are.

Marriage in the First Garden —First Movement

Marriage in the new garden is a clear expression of God's loving nature, just as it was in the first garden of creation. Indeed, the Bible begins (Gen 1:26–28) and ends (Rev 21:9–14) with a wedding. Marriage is so intricately wound into the core theology of Scripture that removing it unravels its integrity. Marriage is first and foremost a portrait of God's identity that he hangs in the entryway of creation's gallery. Accordingly, the primary joy of marriage comes in the fulfillment of God's divine design for creation by the created. Satisfaction in marriage is a by-product of faithfulness to God's call to the covenant of marriage.

This theology of marriage is clearly outlined in the Genesis creation account:

---

31 Bradford Wilcox and Williamson, "Cultural Contradictions," 50.

The Lord God said, "It is not good for the man to be alone. I will make a helper suitable for him." Now the Lord God had formed out of the ground all the wild animals and all the birds in the sky. He brought them to the man to see what he would name them; and whatever the man called each living creature, that was its name. So the man gave names to all the livestock, the birds in the sky and all the wild animals. But for Adam no suitable helper was found. So the Lord God caused the man to fall into a deep sleep; and while he was sleeping, he took one of the man's ribs and then closed up the place with flesh. Then the Lord God made a woman from the rib he had taken out of the man, and he brought her to the man. The man said, "This is now bone of my bones and flesh of my flesh; she shall be called 'woman,' for she was taken out of man." That is why a man leaves his father and mother and is united to his wife, and they become one flesh. (Gen 2:18–24 NIV)

Unfortunately, we have traditionally minimized this narrative through poor interpretation rooted in cultural bias.

The most significant instance in which this is true is the consistent mistranslation of the Hebrew word *tsela* in Genesis 2, which is rendered as "rib" in most English versions of the Bible. While it is possible to understand the word this way, the primary translation of *tsela* is actually "side" or even "half." This word occurs frequently in the Hebrew Scriptures and is translated "side" in every other instance except in Daniel 7:5, in which case the context makes the secondary translation clear. There is no such indication in Genesis 2:21–22, so God really made the woman from half of the man. This certainly changes how we see marriage.

Most of us have always envisioned that God created woman from one of the man's ribs. We can certainly live without a rib or two, but the loss of a side is more profound. What we see here is that God took half of his qualities from the man and formed them into the woman, so that the two halves would create an interdependent whole when bound together. This is why Adam identifies Eve as "bone of his bone and flesh of his flesh." She is the missing half. This also certainly makes sense of Genesis 2:24, the centerpiece of the Bible's theology of marriage: "That

115

is why a man leaves his father and his mother and is united to his wife, and they become one flesh."

That "one flesh" resulting from the reunion of two halves reflects God's very identity in a uniquely holistic way. The Hebrew word that is translated "one" in Genesis 2:24 is *echad*, and this is a relatively rare term in the Old Testament. However, it occurs prominently in the Shema, the central confession of the Hebrew law: "Hear (*shema*), O Israel: the LORD our God, the LORD is one (*echad*)" (Deut 6:4). The word *echad* is richer, by far, than the number one. It conveys a sense of sacred unity, harmony, and wholeness. What cannot be missed here is that the oneness of God is reflected in the oneness of marriage as nowhere else in all of creation. The man and the woman each bring qualities of God to the other as gifts of completion.

Perhaps this also explains the first part of Genesis 2:24—"a man leaves his father and his mother and is united to his wife." In the day Genesis was written (and in the later days of the New Testament, for that matter), the suggestion that a man should leave his parents was utterly countercultural. Traditionally, women would leave their homes when they married and carry their dowries to their husbands' families. A newlywed couple would often add a room to the back of the paternal homeplace and begin their married life there. After all, the husband took his occupation and his livelihood from his father. The creation account makes it clear that the man would spiritually disconnect from his nuclear family in order to bind his life to his wife's.

We often say that human beings are the pinnacle of God's creation, but it may be equally accurate to posit the marriage relationship as the zenith of the first garden. It is not as though God created the man and the woman and left them to discover each other by happenstance, is it? He did not drop them both in the garden and hope that they might fall in love and live happily ever after. God created the man and the woman for each other by making them different from each other and presenting them to each other. He made them a pair, and together they were something they could not be apart: one sacred flesh reflecting his image in covenant relationship.

This is not to suggest, of course, that followers of Christ living singly do not bear the restored image of God in and of themselves. Rather, marriage offers believers a

117

unique opportunity to complete and magnify God's image in relationship. A similar completion occurs in the body of Christ, the church, a correlation Paul acknowledges. Thus, for followers of Christ unrelated through marriage, the familial connection of the local church becomes all the more important to manifesting the image of God. The Creator is nothing if not relational, and he has created us as relational beings in his image. We can serve Christ in singleness, but we cannot serve God alone.

Marriage Lost
—Second Movement

If only the last word on marriage in Genesis were found in chapter 2! Unfortunately, the oneness of marriage is radically disrupted in the sinful fall from God's grace recounted in chapter 3:

> Then the man and his wife heard the sound of the Lord God as he was walking in the garden in the cool of the day, and they hid from the Lord God among the trees of the garden. But the Lord God called to the man, "Where are you?" He answered, "I heard you in the garden, and I was

afraid because I was naked; so I hid." And he said, "Who told you that you were naked? Have you eaten from the tree that I commanded you not to eat from?" The man said, "The woman you put here with me—she gave me some fruit from the tree, and I ate it." Then the Lord God said to the woman, "What is this you have done?" The woman said, "The serpent deceived me, and I ate." (Gen 3:8–13 NIV)

Considering the direct connection of the couple's covenant with God and their covenant with each other, it is not surprising that a breach in the intimate relationship of God and humanity disrupts the intimacy of man and wife. Where once there has been only intimacy and harmony, now there is also enmity and shame. Since the man and the woman no longer recognize God in the same way, they do not recognize the image of God in one another.

Genesis 3 is even more specific about this separation later in the narrative:

To the woman [God] said, "I will make your pains in childbearing very severe; with painful labor you will give birth to children. Your desire

119

will be for your husband, and he will rule over

you." (Gen 3:16 NIV)

Oh, the horror of this utterance from God! Many read it as a punitive injunction, but to us it seems more like a statement of unavoidable consequence. In their newfound selfishness, the woman and the man will still desire each other, but their relationship will be marked by a struggle for control. Even procreation—active participation in God's creative process— will lose much of its wonderment and become painful. There should be no mystery about why marriage is such a complex relationship. It is at the same time so gloriously meaningful and so ingloriously tainted.

This, then, is that state of marriage in a fallen world, another frustratingly marred image of God in desperate need of restoration. For many, marriage has become nothing more than a social or legal contract that can be taken up or discarded for the happiness of the participants. While such freedom would seem to many a key component of happiness, broken marriages seem to be a tremendous source of unhappiness in Western culture. This discontent may well be one result of what prominent American psychologist Barry Schwartz has labelled the "paradox of choice." In his seminal 2004 book, Schwartz draws from a broad array of research to demonstrate that those faced with many desirable choices experience depression and loneliness rather than satisfaction and contentment.[32] When we continue to explore all social and romantic options rather than commit deeply to one spouse for life, we may set ourselves up for a lifetime of discontent. We have high expectations, but we may not commit ourselves to their fulfillment.

Our high expectations for marriage are likely rooted in our sense of what God created marriage to be. Our mistake is believing that the relationship exists merely for our contentment rather than primarily for God's glory. We have painted over the image of God with so many brushstrokes of self-love that we can barely see the magnificence that lies beneath. On June 14, 2014, Brett Zongker of the Associated Press reported that something remarkable had been discovered about Pablo Picasso's first great masterpiece, *The Blue Room* (1901). A conservator at The

---

32 Schwartz, *Paradox of Choice.*

Phillips Collection in Washington, DC, where the painting has resided since 1927, noticed something strange in 1954 when he observed odd brushstrokes in the painting, touches that did not seem consistent with what was visible. In the 1990s, x-rays were able to reveal that something lay underneath, but could not fully reveal what it was. Finally, in 2008, with the benefit of new infrared techniques, scientists were able to see beneath the surface of the painting a hidden image of a bow-tied man with his head resting in his hands. "It's really one of those moments that really makes what you do special," said current conservator Patricia Favero. "The second reaction was, 'Well, who is it?' We're still working on answering that question."[33]

Perhaps what makes conflicted marriages so frustrating is that those in them intuit that they should and could be something much more than social contracts or relational quests for happiness. They observe odd brushstrokes that cause them to suspect a greater end and higher purpose. Something is hidden beneath, something mysterious and deep, but they cannot see

33 Zongker, "Picasso Painting Reveals Hidden Man."

Submit to one another out of reverence for Christ. Wives, submit yourselves to your own husbands as you do to the Lord. For the husband is the head of the wife as Christ is the head of the church, his body, of which he is the Saviour. Now as the church submits to Christ, so also wives should submit to their husbands in everything. Husbands, love your wives, just as Christ loved the church and gave himself up for her to make her holy, cleansing her by the washing with water through the word, and to present her to himself as a radiant church, without stain or wrinkle or any other blemish, but holy and blameless. In this same way, husbands ought to love their wives as their own bodies. He who loves his wife loves himself. After all, no one ever hated their own body, but they feed and care for their body, just as Christ does the church—for we are members of his body. "For this reason a man will leave his father and mother and be united to his wife, and the two will become one flesh." This is a profound mystery—but I am talking about Christ and the church. However, each one of you also must love his wife as he loves himself, and the wife must respect her husband.

(Eph 5:21–33 NIV)

What the apostle Paul describes in this passage is marriage as it has been re-created in the new garden. He calls husbands and wives back to a covenant of mutual submission out of reverence for the new gardener.

Paul draws attention away from the rights and selfish needs of husbands and wives and toward their covenant responsibilities. Still, the two halves of God's nature are strangely completed in the marriage he commends. The husband especially receives the respect he longs for and for the wife there is also adoration to her heart's content. This unification is so complete that Paul seems almost to become confused about whether he is speaking about the covenant of marriage or the covenant between Christ and his church. In the end, he is speaking about both. In either case, the union created by God between the one and the other is so profound that it mystifies Paul and us.

It is in this context of marriage created by God in the first garden and now re-created in Christ's resurrection for the second that we must consider the sexual ethic of the New

Testament. Within the covenant of marriage, sex is both a means of procreation and a powerful agent binding the man and his wife. G. K. Chesterton stated this reality well:

> Sex is an instinct that produces an institution; and it is positive and not negative, noble and not base, creative and not destructive, because it produces this institution. That institution is the family; a small state or commonwealth which has hundreds of aspects, when it is once started, that are not sexual at all. It includes worship, justice, festivity, decoration, instruction, comradeship, repose. Sex is the gate of that house; and romantic and imaginative people naturally like looking through a gateway. But the house is very much larger than the gate. There are indeed a certain number of people who like to hang about the gate and never get any further.[34]

The full counsel of the Bible is that God established sex for this sacred purpose. When exercised according to God's plan in marriage, sexual expression is a fulfillment of God's perfect plan for humanity.

---

34 Chesterton, *G.K.'s Weekly.*

The consistent witness of the Bible is thus that God created human sexual expression exclusively for the marriage of the man and his wife. C. S. Lewis, who lived in singleness much of his life, offered as much when he wrote, "The monstrosity of sexual intercourse outside of marriage is that those who indulge in it are trying to isolate one kind of union (the sexual) from all the other kinds of union which were intended to go along with it and make up the total union."[35]

Sexual expression outside of the marriage covenant is like playing with fire. It is exciting, but those involved do not understand the power they are touching. Like fire, sex as God created it is an essential force for good when properly contained in the covenant of marriage, but a destructive force when uncontained. Those who misuse sex are bound to get burned.

In the new garden of the resurrection, sex is restored as a powerful tie that binds the man to his wife. As we are re-created in Christ's resurrection, we recover the power of sex in

35 Lewis, *Mere Christianity*, 96.

RISE | Reimagining the Resurrection Life

marriage and put aside sexual expressions that produce shame and brokenness. Paul is very practical in his teaching on this subject, noting the powerful implications for believers:

> By his power God raised the Lord from the dead, and he will raise us also. Do you not know that your bodies are members of Christ himself? Shall I then take the members of Christ and unite them with a prostitute? Never! Do you not know that he who unites himself with a prostitute is one with her in body? For it is said, "The two will become one flesh." But whoever is united with the Lord is one with him in spirit. Flee from sexual immorality. All other sins a person commits are outside the body, but whoever sins sexually, sins against their own body. (1 Cor 6:14–18 NIV)

Note in this passage the apostle's direct connection of sexuality to the Bible's central ethos of marriage: "The two will become one flesh." He wisely counsels that sex outside of the marriage covenant dangerously unites entities in ways God never intended. This not only dishonors God, but also damages God's people.

I often teach my parishioners that sex is the superglue of marriage. A fan of the chemical bonding agent (cyanoacrylate), I know by experience that superglue bonds things together instantly, sometimes in unintended ways. When used correctly, superglue creates a desirable attachment. But I cannot count for the number of times I have glued myself to something I was seeking to repair, tearing away skin in the process. Likewise, sex is a powerful bonding agent of husband and wife. That is what God created it to be, which is why it is also so dangerous when used counter to God's intent. When we employ sexual expression inside our bodies but outside of God's will, we dangerously bind our souls to whatever we touch, whether pornography, commercial products, prostitutes, or casual partners.

Living in the new garden, though, we are free to enjoy sexual expression in marriage entirely without shame. Having recovered its purpose as a sacred bond between husband and wife, we are able to put aside any negativity we might have associated with sex in the past. As Richard Neuhaus celebrates:

Sexual satisfaction is closely related to the absence of sexual anxiety. One reason the faithfully married have an easier time with intimacy is that they enjoy greater sexual freedom. Not sexual freedom in the sense in which the term is commonly used, including the freedom to sleep around. Rather, they have greater sexual freedom in the sense of freedom from the anxieties that bedevil sex for many, if not most, who are not monogamous. They are free, inter alia, from guilt about violating their own sense of morality, free from fear of sexually transmitted diseases, free from fear of out-of-wedlock pregnancy, free from fear of comparison to other partners, and free from fear of losing the partner to another. Taken all in all, it looks much more like sexual freedom than what is called sexual freedom.[36]

As in all instances, the restoration of the resurrection means real freedom for those re-created in Christ. As countercultural as it sounds to say so, a lifelong marriage commitment is a gift of liberty from the Creator offered anew in Christ.

---

36 Richard Neuhaus, cited in Gold, *God, Love, Sex, and Family,* 187.

Marriages of the new creation are those that honor God and present an accurate portrayal of his love within his creation. Marriage is restored as a portrait of God's identity that he hangs in the entryway of creation's gallery. As such, it exists for the benefit of the creation as for the benefit of any human couple. A good marriage is a gift both to God, to any children it produces, and to the broader community. The author of Hebrews underscores the broad functionality of marriage in the new garden when he writes:

> Marriage should be honored by all, and the marriage bed kept pure, for God will judge the adulterer and all the sexually immoral. Keep your lives free from the love of money and be content with what you have, because God has said, "Never will I leave you; never will I forsake you." So we say with confidence, "The Lord is my helper; I will not be afraid. What can mere mortals do to me?" (Heb 13:4–6 NIV)

Not to be missed in this passage is sound advice about the two issues of ten indicated as the sources of greatest conflict in marriage: sex and money. But the most powerful dictate of this

Scripture is that marriage is to be honored by everyone. Even if we are not married, we are to respect and preserve marriage as the image of the Creator. If we are married, then our responsibility to protect the purity of the relationship is profound.

Perhaps Hebrews 13 also offers us the best news about marriage in the new creation: God is ever-present in the relationship! No mere mortal can destroy it. As the traditional intonation goes, "What God hath joined together, let no person lay asunder." Restored to the relationship God created to procreate his world and represent the whole of his nature, we learn that "The Lord is [our] helper; [we] will not be afraid." This is the hopeful promise of marriage in the new garden.

Living in the New Garden —Fourth Movement

Just revisioning marriage as God has re-created it in the resurrection of Jesus Christ can shift significantly the quality of our marriage relationships. However, there are some obvious implications of resurrection theology for our marriages as we live in the new garden. First, we must learn not only to accept but also to appreciate the distinctions each spouse brings to the relationship. These include gender distinctives, strengths, and healthy personality traits. Too many husbands and wives either reject or merely put up with the distinctives in their spouses, making it difficult for the tolerated spouse to really experience love in the home. By God's design, marriage is not a relationship of sameness, but of completion. This is why we so often say, "opposites attract," but we might be far better served by telling the stories of our marriages as relationships in which "complements complete." The irony, of course, is that we generally initiate an effort to remake our spouse in our own images before we even say, "I do." The moment we succeed in quashing the uniqueness of the other in marriage, we disrupt the fullness of God's image in the relationship and experience boredom and complacency.

A second inference is that husband and wife each bear personal responsibility for bringing the restored image of God to the relationship through their individual discipleship. In other words, each spouse must incarnate Christ's resurrection personally in order to hope to find the wholeness of God's image completed in the other. A husband cannot seek validation in his wife, nor a wife in her husband. Only God can validate us through the Holy Spirit as his beloved children adopted through Christ's resurrection. In the new garden, we must always seek to come to one another authentically re-created by the Holy Spirit, bringing our strength to each relationship as a sacred offering both to God and to the other. The work of the Holy Spirit is to replicate the identity of the risen Lord in us. The work of the spouse is to complement and affirm that identity through the covenant of marriage.

Third, our marriage journeys are deeply connected to our spiritual journeys. More often than not, as goes one, so goes the other. We began this chapter with an indication that marriages planted actively in the life of churches were more likely to survive. We would offer further that couples who actively seek God together daily are more likely to thrive. This capacity has too often been distilled into rote daily Scripture reading and prayer. While these disciplines are certainly important for couples in Christ, we think there is more to resurrection marriage than that. We would suggest that couples work together to create sacred space in their lives together. Recover the sanctuary of the supper table, the liturgy of intimate conversation, and the sacrament of the marriage bed. God created marriage to be a transformational relationship, and it loses its purpose when it becomes a continuous loop of transaction. Find the image of God in the worship of marriage.

Finally, we can learn to enjoy our marriage relationships in all of their complexities, and then offer them to the world as portraits of God's love. Either marriage in the new garden is a joyful experience, or it is still waiting to be fully resurrected. Couples in Christ are invited to really appreciate each other as physical and spiritual lovers. So sings the husband in the Song of Songs, "How beautiful you are, my darling! Oh, how beautiful! Your eyes are doves." And so replies his wife, "How handsome you are, my beloved! Oh, how charming! And our bed is verdant" (Song 1:15–16 NIV). And so says God, "The two shall become one flesh."

CHAPTER 6:

REST AND SABBATH

So also, when we were underage, we were in slavery under the elemental spiritual forces of the world. But when the set time had fully come, God sent his Son, born of a woman, born under the law, to redeem those under the law, that we might receive adoption to sonship. Because you are his sons, God sent the Spirit of his Son into our hearts, the Spirit who calls out, "Abba, Father." So you are no longer a slave, but God's child; and since you are his child, God has made you also an heir. Formerly, when you did not know God, you were slaves to those who by nature are not gods. But now that you know God—or rather are known by God—how is it that you are turning back to those weak and miserable forces? Do you wish to be enslaved by them all over again? You are observing special days and months and seasons and years! I fear for you, that somehow I have wasted my efforts on you. (Gal 4:3–11 NIV)

That is the grandeur and the sorrow of the white, middle-class, heterosexual man. He does his duty. He is alarmed awake in the morning earlier than his system is ready for. He bolts his breakfast and runs for a crowded filthy train. He poisons his spirit with the newspaper because he is a responsible citizen and is morally obliged to keep in touch with the latest disasters from home and abroad. He endures a day tied to a desk or a lathe deferring to a boss he despises. He counts the days to his long-service leave and his early retirement package. He is without realising it, a true epicurean philosopher—he limits his desires in the hope of diminishing the

138

misery of frustration. He tries not to alarm his
family with the announcement that he's chucked
the job and intends to pop over to Nepal for a
spot of mountaineering while he still has the
legs for it. He keeps his trap shut and keeps his
dreams to himself.[37]

In our workaholic, frantic paced world rest does not come easily for most. Even those who have retired tell us they are busier than they have ever been. As if being busy means therefore, I am fine! Technology, laptops, and smartphones mean we are constantly on call. The office goes with us! Downtime and solitude do not even exist as we travel! On buses, trains, and at airports smartphones and iPods work overtime. It reminds us of Billy Joel's tag song, "Piano Man," where the businessmen, sailor, and real estate agent cry, "sing us a song you're the piano man . . . to forget about life for a while." And this twenty-first-century lifestyle extends beyond work. Kids sport throws all the family into the chaos of frantically travelling from field to field then

---

37 Lane, *Good Weekend.*

home again for the next installment. We can find our identity and validation in our busyness with rest being an uneasy notion.

I was asked to speak at a church anniversary and the senior minister pleaded, "speak on a topic that's not the norm." So, I chose, "Being Restful for God." When I arrived at the church the sign out the front said, "Today's Sermon: Being Active for God." I challenged the minister about the sign. "Oh, no," he replied, "We thought you had inadvertently conveyed the wrong message, as we are committed disciples here." Even after the sermon, he did not get it, although from responses his people did. Christianity for him was all transactions, no rest! Life in the garden was not meant to be that way. Rest is a foundational component of discipleship. In *Moby Dick*, Captain Ahab has the harpooners resting whilst the other crew row frantically. Why, because he knows those who are harpooners must raise to their feet out of rest, not out of toil. To be a follower of Christ is to be a harpooner!

There is more to rest than just restoring the spirit for what lies ahead. In her Australian outback novel, *The Promise of Rain*, Gail Morgan has this poignant exchange between two

140

central characters. "The priest said to the other, 'To do nothing in someone's presence is a greater compliment than being busy.'" Don't we know that? To just be with one's partner, children or friends is the best. To spend leisurely time by the BBQ, at a game, reading books together, not being rushed but enjoying life with others is the greatest complement we can pay each other. Do we "do nothing" in the presence of our God? Jesus spent quality time with his Father and the disciples. He "hangs out" with his disciples, walked the hills of Galilee, and rose early to be alone with the one he loved. The apostle Mark records, "Very early in the morning, while it was still dark, Jesus got up, left the house, and went off to a solitary place, where he prayed" (Mark 1:35 NIV).

The success of the author John Grisham is not just because he is a superb legal thriller storyteller. More often than not, the insanely busy lawyer, chasing billable hours, abandons that to go sailing or to find the job where she or he can spend time being human and enjoying life out of the rat race. This makes his novels a catharsis for the holiday reader who dreams of a release from a meaningless life of busyness.

Rest in the First Garden
—First Movement

What is "rest?" Biblically, is it just a lack of a frantic activity? We need to look closely at how Genesis portrays the seventh day in the garden of Eden:

> Thus the heavens and the earth were completed in all their vast array. By the seventh day God had finished the work he had been doing; so on the seventh day he rested from all his work. Then God blessed the seventh day and made it holy, because on it he rested from all the work of creating that he had done." (Gen 2:1–3 NIV)

What takes one by surprise here is that there is no actual mention of the Sabbath. We do read that God ceased his creation, translated "rest," but the context is not of God "laying down tools" for good, rather that he is well pleased and satisfied. The rest of achievement one could say. In fact, Jesus would go on to declare, "My Father is still working" (John 5:17). This no doubt refers to his Father fulfilling his plan of salvation and cosmic purposes. There is also a sense of his ongoing nurture of the garden as we see in Genesis 3:21 when he made garments of skin for Adam and Eve.

The picture in the first garden is very different to the one revealed in the creation stories of the non-Abrahamic world. Their gods are completely freed from their labors as humanity was created for the sole purpose of carrying out the desires of the deities. Our God is not self-consumed or inactive.

God then blesses the seventh day as holy. What God has done on the previous six days he declares as good. Now we have the seventh day. It is good. This seventh day is what the creation order was meant to be. There is no other day to come, as the formula that is mentioned for the other six days of creation, "and there was evening and there was morning," is absent. This seventh day was to be infinite with no beginning or end. The fact that God has blessed and sanctified it means it is not for God alone but all creation. The day climaxes in a perfect relationship horizontally between God and us, and vertically between humanity and the rest of the created order. This is the shalom of Scripture. It is beautifully described by Christian philosopher Nicholas Wolterstorff:

143

Shalom is the human being dwelling at peace in all his or her relationships: with God, with self, with fellow, with nature . . . But the peace which is shalom is not merely the absence of hostility, not merely being in right relationship. Shalom at its highest is enjoyment in one's relationships . . . To dwell in shalom is to enjoy living before God, to enjoy living in one's physical surroundings, to enjoy living with one's fellows, to enjoy living with oneself.[38]

This shalom goal of creation rest in which humanity would "rule" and "subdue" fruitfully under God has not been abandoned. The Bible promises that the children of Israel are to find this rest in the promised land. For followers of Jesus, it is a future hope that breaks into our everyday world and is the inauguration of Christ's resurrection reign (Heb 3–4:7). The writer of Hebrews records that under Moses the children of Israel did not enter his rest. However, if we, unlike them, "hear his voice" and "do not

---

38 Wolterstorff, *Justice and Peace,* 69–70.

harden our hearts" the promise of "entering his rest still stands"
(Heb 3:7—4:7).

Rest Lost
—Second Movement

A world devoid of the seventh day of rest is outlined in the
fall. God orders,

> Cursed is the ground because of you; through
> painful toil you will eat food from it all the days
> of your life. It will produce thorns and thistles
> for you and you will eat the plants of the field.
> By the sweat of your brow you will eat your food
> until you return to the ground, since from it you
> were taken; for dust you are and to dust you will
> return. (Gen 3:17b–19)

How quickly we read over God's sentence on humanity that this
predicament will be for "all the days of your life." Ecclesiastes
expresses over and over the "vanity" of such living.

> As everyone comes, so they depart, and what
> do they gain, since they toil for the wind? All

145

their days they eat in darkness, with great
frustration, affliction and anger . . . For who
knows what is good for a person in life, during
the few and meaningless days they pass through
like a shadow? Who can tell them what will
happen under the sun after they are gone? (Eccl
5:16b–17; 6:12)

God does not leave his covenant people to this brokenness and
dysfunctionality. In Exodus 16:21–30 the word Sabbath first
appears. It is a transliteration, not translation, of the Hebrew
word for "cursed" in Genesis 2:1–3, "sabbat." People ceased
work on the seventh day (v. 30). It is a "holy Sabbath to the Lord"
and the baking of food and the like is to occur on the sixth day.
This concept of Sabbath becomes the fourth commandment:

Remember the Sabbath day by keeping it holy.
Six days you shall labour and do all your work,
but the seventh day is a sabbath to the LORD
your God. On it you shall not do any work,
neither you, nor your son or daughter, nor your
male or female servant, nor your animals, nor
any foreigner residing in your towns. For in six
days the LORD made the heavens and the earth,

146

> the sea, and all that is in them, but he rested on
> the seventh day. Therefore the LORD blessed the
> Sabbath day and made it holy. (Exod 20:8–11)

We believe this is not the perfect shalom of the first garden. Verse 11 is a quotation of Genesis 2:3 but "seventh" now reads "Sabbath." Surely this alteration binds the two days closely together, but it does not make them one. The purpose here is not to show that the two days are equal in every respect, "but rather to show that God's action of blessing and sanctifying applies equally to both. Verse 11b is a shorthand way of saying, 'which is why Yahweh blessed not only the seventh day, but also the Sabbath.'"[39] In the fourth commandment what we have is a type of memorial for what was, plus a time set aside to celebrate the goodness of God and his creation away from the cycle of toilsome existence brought by the fall.

In Deuteronomy, Moses preached the law to God's chosen people. With respect to the Sabbath, the instruction is to observe the commandment already received in the Exodus (Deut 5:12–15). Moses then expanded on the fourth commandment and

---

39 Shead, "Sabbath," 746.

decreed it to be a day for all to equally share in no matter their status in society. It was also a day to remember God's liberating grace in that he brought Israel out of bondage towards the promised land; a covenant sign of God's ongoing goodness to his people and their redemption (Gen 32:12–17).

The Sabbath continues as a sacred day of assembly throughout the Old Testament, with harsh penalties for those who willfully abuse it (Jer 19–23).

Rest in the New Garden —Third Movement

If we were surprised by the fact that there was no mention of an actual Sabbath in the first garden, we will be equally surprised that there is no commandment or instruction to keep the Sabbath in the new garden. Resurrection living is not Sabbath keeping. Unlike the early church, tragically from the time of Emperor Constantine's adoption of Christianity in the fourth century, the church has often sought to massage the rules and regulations of the Old Testament Sabbath to make them applicable and amenable to the follower of Christ. But we are people restored to the first garden. It is the pre-fall, not post-fall seventh day that the risen Christ draws us to. God's rest is a glorious eschatological hope that fully embraces at least all of the first garden (Rev 21:3–5), yet the morning has broken. Justo L. Gonzales states that for the early church Sunday was not a day of sobriety or regulation but a day of "joy and celebration, connected first of all with the resurrection of Jesus, but also with the beginning of the new creation."[40]

Jesus as the new Adam is our prototype. He lived perfectly the life we are called to live. Stephen Neill counsels, "Christian perfection is not the observance of a code of moral rules, or the avoidance of transgression, or an inner state of devotion—though all these things may enter into it. It is a manifestation of the conquering power of Christ in every situation and in every relationship of human life."[41] The religious leaders of that day did not appreciate this truth about Jesus's life or calling. He is accused by the religious leaders of Sabbath breaking. His

---

40 For discussion see Gonzales, *Brief History.*

41 Neill, *Christian Holiness*, 42.

disciples were hungry, and they began to pick and eat grain as Jesus led them temptingly through the grain fields (Matt 12:1–2). Jesus goes on to confront his accusers:

> Haven't you read what David did when he and his companions were hungry? He entered the house of God, and he and his companions ate the consecrated bread—which was not lawful for them to do, but only for the priests. Or haven't you read in the Law that the priests on Sabbath duty in the temple desecrate the Sabbath and yet are innocent? I tell you that something greater than the temple is here. If you had known what these words mean, "I desire mercy, not sacrifice"; you would not have condemned the innocent. For the Son of Man is Lord of the Sabbath. (Matt 12:3–8 NIV)

Jesus responds by saying that he is not breaking the law but fulfilling it. Just as he promised in the Sermon on the Mount, he came not to "abolish" the law but to fulfill it (Matt 5:17–18). Jesus has the authority to reclaim and restate the seventh day as he has just declared that in him we find our rest and comfort (Matt 11:28–30). The incarnate one is on the journey to death, resurrection, and exaltation. Shead states, "Jesus' taking authority over the Sabbath both wrest it from the legal framework in which it previously stood and realizes the rest which God's people were always intended to enjoy."[42] Not only does this imply that Jesus has an authority at least as great as that of the Mosaic law, it suggests that Jesus is the one who will finally bring the blessings of the Sabbath to Israel.[43]

As often is the case the Synoptic Gospels go on to illustrate Jesus's teaching with one of his miracles. The next scene in Matthew's Gospel is the synagogue. Jesus provocatively asked, "is it lawful to heal on the Sabbath?" Then he said to a disabled man, "Stretch out your hand." So the man stretched out his hand and "it was completely restored, just as sound as the other." A familiar story unfolds in Luke's Gospel as a disabled woman is healed on the Sabbath. This teaching and application became too much for the Pharisees and they "went out and plotted how they might kill Jesus" (Matt 12:13–14).

---

42 Shead, "Sabbath," 748.

43 Shead, "Sabbath," 748.

151

Jesus is the Lord of the Sabbath. In him is the restoration of shalom: well-being. The religious authorities of his day—and in some cases ours—did not get it! Jesus brings the blessings of liberation and salvation of the first garden's seventh day to a fractured world. The apostle Paul sums this up magnificently:

> Therefore do not let anyone judge you by what you eat or drink, or with regard to a religious festival, a New Moon celebration or a Sabbath day. These are a shadow of the things that were to come; the reality, however, is found in Christ. (Col 2:16–17 NIV)

Living in the New Garden —Fourth Movement

The restoration of "rest" in Christ does not mean there is no place for the seven-day cycle. Certainly, there is benefit in maintaining, in a non-legalistic way, a cycle of six days of work and the seventh one of rest, as our world is still fractured. In our modern world, the timing and structure of such a day will differ from family to family, and community to community. This cycle of rest benefits the animal world and the fields as well as humans (Lev 25:1–7). This weekly paradigm has been proven to provide humanity with the pattern of work and the recharging of mind, body, and spirit that is so desperately needed for healthy living. And there is significant research on how important a seven-day cycle is for pastors and church leaders. Flabby, obese ministers can be a connection to a non-stop ministry life.[44]

John Ortberg has raised the bar on the reimplementation of Sabbath rest as part of healthy spiritual formation.[45] Church leaders must model healthy rest, and a God-honoring cycle of life.[46]

Yet the real restoration of the seventh day is much deeper than the "Sabbath." It is the enactment of shalom. It is about justice and liberation for all. In the first garden God rests as his creation was all that it could be. It was harmonious. Constantly, we must remind ourselves that the "Sabbath" is a gift of God for human flourishing. It is an opportunity for the people of God to

---

44 Gleanings, *Why Protestants Need Rest,* 14.

45 Ortberg, *Soul Keeping.*

46 See Bruggerman, *Sabbath as Resistance.*

imitate the God of freedom in the ways in which we structure our lives and communities. Sabbath functions as a tacit indictment of all those social structures and human systems that do not mirror God's shalom. It is intended as a gift to all—including the most vulnerable and those whose toil drives the wheels of production. It is a warning to those who oversee systems that keep people enslaved that they will be called to account. They are reminded that they will pass, and will have no role in the goal toward which God is taking the creation.[47]

There is an eschatological perspective that deepens our understanding of rest in the new garden. God's last word in the Bible (Rev 21–22) informs us that when Jesus comes again, the new garden will not just duplicate the old. In these two chapters, the image is not just of a garden but a "garden city." There is a holy city, the new Jerusalem in the midst of the river and trees (Rev 21:2—22:1–2).

Why are we given this picture of a garden city? Because the ancient world, like ours, was one of cities. Cities, despite

---

47 Sloane, "Peace in Our Time."

the fall, represent something of the development of human civilization. Humans have produced much (Job 28). The new garden will not just embrace all that is good in the first instance, but will take, renew, and transform all of civilization. Our "rest" to come is not located in some idealistic rural outpost but is eternally lived out in the vibrancy of a garden city. A city of work, play, and retreat—all that is best. It is that rest that breaks in now. Jürgen Moltmann puts it this way:

> As the perfect city, it fulfills the history of human
> civilization, which according to the biblical
> saga began when Cain, the city-builder (Gen.
> 4:17), murdered his brother Abel, the nomadic
> shepherd. The New Jerusalem holds within itself
> the Garden of Eden (Rev. 22:1ff) and is an image
> of perfect harmony between civilization and
> nature. It thereby also consummates the history
> of earthly nature with human beings. The city of
> God lives in nature, and nature lives in the city
> of God. "The garden city" was an ancient ideal
> of the polis for many peoples.[48]

---

48 Moltmann, *Coming of God.*

God the Creator was present in the first garden, not just some absent landlord. He watches over Adam and Eve, speaks with them, and they hear him walking in the garden (Gen 1:28; 2:16–17, 3:8–13). The image in Revelation heightens the intensity of God's presence. We are his "bride," he "dwells" with us, he wipes away our tears, and he is our light (Rev 21:2–4; 22:4). His protection now is absolute. There is no death because of his abundant presence (Rev 21:4). And even more significantly, God is now fully revealed as the Trinitarian God: Father, Son, and Holy Spirit. There is a richness in the names of God: Alpha and Omega, the Lamb, the Spirit, the one who satisfies our thirst. As some scholars like to say, the picture in Revelation is the presence of this God in the "space" of his created beings. God is truly Immanuel: in our midst. This is so much more than the picture given in Genesis 1 and 2. The new garden embraces all of Genesis but our "rest" is now intimately with the Gardener himself. That is the rest we now in part experience in Christ, as we live in the new garden and await its consummation.

What are some of the implications in light of the above for resurrection living? The goal of resurrection discipleship is not

156

just instructional but the shaping of our lives, relationships, and communities. In our everyday lives work and busyness are not to be worshipped or to be the foundation of our significance. True worship and significance are found in resting in the triune God, through the risen Christ. It is a holistic life of celebrating the goodness of creation, a balance between work and recreation, that contemporary society needs to see modelled. As Brother Jeremiah retorted, "If I had my life to live over, I would start barefooted earlier in the spring and stay that way later in the fall. I would play more. I would ride on more merry-go-rounds. I'd pick more daisies."[49]

In church life, there is the temptation of busyness. We find a practical way of finding a balance in the "three ones." Church members are encouraged to be involved in one worship service, one small group, and one area of service. They are not to consume their life with more and more activity. As one pastor said, "his greatest fear is he wouldn't go to his own church." Why? Because he said, "he feared it would consume him to a

---

49 Recorded in Engstrom, *Pursuit of Excellence*, 90.

point of burn out or dropping out of church life." This is not a picture of shalom or "doing nothing" with God, friends, and family that is part of true humanity. It is contrary to the story of Mary and Martha (Luke 10:38–42). Martha finds her authentic life in busyness and she has an honorable goal; to physically feed Jesus and his team. Yet Mary avoids all the cooking and serving tasks at hand and just sits at the feet of her master, being with him and listening. To sit at the feet is a symbol of homage and worship. Martha's annoyance explodes into the cry, "Lord, don't you care that my sister has left me to do the work by myself? Tell her to help me!" The Lord of the Sabbath, the new garden, the seventh day, does no such thing. "Martha, Martha," the Lord answered, "you are worried and upset about many things, but few things are needed—or indeed only one. Mary has chosen what is better, and it will not be taken away from her" (Luke 10:41–42). The Lord's rebuke is not over Martha's lack of grace and her raised voice, as some claim. It is over the fact that she has not embraced transformative discipleship.

We know what it is like to be Martha. Late one Saturday, I started to mow my lawn. Darkness was descending but I had little option as close friends and family were coming for lunch the next day for a big family get together. I had filled the week with so many church activities and acts of Christian service that the untidy, long grass could only now be attended to. As there was little natural light left, I put on outside lights and started to mow. The next door neighbor's light went on and I could see eyes peer through a window. Then, like the old Flintstones television show, lights went on in houses up and down the street. Neighbors were checking out who the man was that needed to mow his lawn in the dark on a Saturday night. The Lord spoke to me and the message was clear—you have "killed" your witness in Bradley Road tonight. Who would want to be involved in a way of life that is so immersed in endless activity that they even mow their lawn in the dark?

It is time for the disciples of Jesus to follow the way of the master and practice seventh-day creation life. That is seven days a week! God has made this material world for his glory and our enjoyment. A day to be well satisfied with our work, leisure, family life, and service. It is good! The seventh day is life God's way. It is time to refocus:

Life from the centre is a life of unhurried peace and power. It is simple. It is serene. It is amazing. It is triumphant. It is radiant. It takes no time, but it occupies all our time. And it makes our life programs new and overcoming. We need not get frantic. He is at the helm. And when our little day is done, we lie down quietly in peace, for all is well.[50]

---

50 Kelly, *Testament of Devotion*, 104.

CHAPTER 7:

STEWARDSHIP AND

CREATION CARE

Then I saw "a new heaven and a new earth," for the first heaven and the first earth had passed away, and there was no longer any sea. I saw the Holy City, the new Jerusalem, coming down out of heaven from God, prepared as a bride beautifully dressed for her husband. And I heard a loud voice from the throne saying, "Look! God's dwelling place is now among the people, and he will dwell with them. They will be his people, and God himself will be with them and be their God. 'He will wipe every tear from their eyes. There will be no more death' or mourning or crying or pain, for the old order of things has passed away." (Rev 21:1–4 NIV)

At the beginning as well as at the end of the religious history of man, we find the same yearning for Paradise. If we take into account the fact that the yearning for Paradise is equally discernible in the general religious attitude of early man, we have the right to assume that the mystical memory of blessedness with history haunts man from the moment he becomes aware of his situation in the cosmos.[51]

We live in a day where there is a true longing for a return to the creation order of Genesis 1–2, a place where humanity respects, preserves, and cares for all the good things of the world. This yearning for restoration of the created order is not just seen in the church.

---

51 Eliade, "Yearning for Paradise," 73.

On a visit to Russia, I was asked to give talks at a number of universities and to enter into a time of sharing and dialogue. To my amazement, the most frequently asked question by the students was whether the resurrected Jesus would bring the utopia that Marxism had failed to deliver. Even Gorbachev, and the regimes that followed, has failed us, was the cry. The human longing for a new world order had not been met in these students' aspirations.

There is a cosmic dream that sparks hope and a wish for more. It is not just found in Marxism. Gaia is the name of the ancient Greek goddess of the earth. Gaia has become a popular mythological symbol that unites many who care about the environment. For Gaia, the whole of planet earth is not merely interconnected but is a living, and for some a divine, being. Figuratively it's a new day, a dawning, the "Age of Aquarius," and together we must work for it now. Gaia is further evidence that longing for a return to paradise lost is not divorced from one's spiritual journey.

Our next-door neighbors may well embrace such an ideal, whether they belong to a "green consciousness" movement,

New Spiritualities or just want to link with those who live out creation care.

We believe for followers of Jesus that an "evacuation" theology is not enough. Life is more than simply giving your heart to Jesus and awaiting the rapture or eternal life. The resurrection of Jesus calls us to live with the vision of a re-created eternal garden. With that vision motivating our own stewardship we start to witness its dawning, as we await its final fulfillment in Jesus's return. Resurrection living is clearly a foretaste of heaven on earth. Isaiah the prophet eloquently pictures the vision:

> See, I will create new heavens and a new earth. The former things will not be remembered, nor will they come to mind. But be glad and rejoice forever in what I will create, for I will create Jerusalem to be a delight and its people a joy . . . The wolf and the lamb will feed together, and the lion will eat straw like the ox, and dust will be the serpent's food. They will neither harm nor destroy on all my holy mountain, says the LORD. (Isa 65:17–18, 25 NIV)

Stewardship in the First Garden —First Movement

As a consequence of being in the divine image, Adam and Eve exercised stewardship. In the ancient Near East, the raising of a king's statue was equivalent to declaring him lord over the immediate area. Humanity is created in God's image and therefore as God's "statue" represent his rule over all creation. Genesis 1:26 and 28 states, "then God said, Let us make mankind in our image, in our likeness, so that they may rule over the fish in the sea and the birds in the sky, over the livestock and all the wild animals, and over all the creatures that move along the ground . . . God blessed them and said to them, 'Be fruitful and increase in number; fill the earth and subdue it. Rule over the fish in the sea and the birds in the sky and over every living creature that moves on the ground.'" Psalm 8 stresses the same truth: that humanity is God's ruler over God's world.

In the first garden, "rule" (or as it is sometimes translated, "dominion"), and "subdue" did not represent exploitation of creation. The rule was over all creation, including all major

165

zoological groups. The reformer John Calvin demonstrates the spirit of what God intended:

> The earth was given to man with this condition, that he should occupy himself in its cultivation . . . The custody of the garden was given in charge to Adam, to show that we possess the things that God has committed to our hands, on the condition that being content with frugal and moderate use of them, we should take care of what shall remain . . . Let everyone regard himself as the steward of God in all things which he possesses. Then will he neither conduct himself dissolutely, nor corrupt by abuse those things which God requires to be preserved.[52]

In God's garden, all of creation is good. There is harmony between humans and an interconnection with all living creatures. Adam and Eve were given the responsibility as image bearers and are held accountable as caretakers for God's handiwork (Gen 2:15). Old Testament scholar, Kenneth A. Matthews, indicates that this perception of the creation narrative led to the Hebrew love

---

52 Calvin, *Commentary on Genesis.*

of life and the belief that "the sacredness of all life assume[s] a linkage between righteousness and the welfare of the earth."[53]

In the garden God is a provider and ensures food for humanity and the animal world but not in a cruel, exploitative way.

> Then God said, "I give you every seed-bearing plant on the face of the whole earth and every tree that has fruit with seed in it. They will be yours for food. And to all the beasts of the earth and all the birds in the sky and all the creatures that move along the ground—everything that has the breath of life in it—I give every green plant for food." And it was so. God saw all that he had made, and it was very good. And there was evening, and there was morning—the sixth day. (Gen 1:29–31 NIV)

As the writer of proverbs expanded, "A righteous man cares for the needs of his animals" (Prov 12:10a). With respect to resources, the biblical ideal is to meet proper human needs for building materials, and for instruments of play, but not for

---

53 Matthews, *Genesis 1–11:26*, 175.

indiscriminate use that rapes the environment (Job 28). All of creation is precious! It was a place of peace and perfection.

On occasions, followers of Jesus have jumped on words like "rule" and "subdue" to justify indifference to creation. One church leader put on Facebook words to the effect that he would drive his SUV across sand dunes, fields or whatever and burn up barrels of fuel as he "ruled." God was coming back to restore it all anyway! Such sentiments totally distort Genesis 1:28 which is a foundation for creation care and environmental ethics and is not a command to "rough ride" over all of God's handiwork. This Genesis command to rule follows the Bible's statement about the creation of Adam and Eve in God's image. They are his "statue" and are to replicate his holiness and wisdom. And we know God adores all of creation. As Collins points out, words like "subdue" and "rule" are in the context of the immense and trusted task God has given humanity in the first garden. Creation is enormous and awesome, and it will take all of Adam and Eve's "energy of strength" and wisdom. Collins continues, "Mankind's original task was to begin from Eden, work their way outward, and spread the blessings of Eden to all the earth. This would mean managing all of its creatures and resources for good purposes: to allow their beauty to flourish, to use them wisely and kindly, and to promote well-being of all."[54]

It is in this context one understands the meaning of "rule" and "subdue." It describes the task ahead of humanity, which is to be carried out consistently with God's purposes and his glory.

Godly stewardship in the first garden was a core concept for practicing a holy life. Stewardship was a gift of God's grace to Adam and Eve. It was to reflect his glory in all creation, whether that be our relationship with the animal kingdom, the environment or each other. The gift was to be administered faithfully towards all that was good in the first garden.

Stewardship Lost
—Second Movement

Genesis 3 dramatically reveals the extent of creation's fall as a result of our sin and shame. It corrupts every aspect of our environment and life together. Good stewardship, including

---

54 Collins, *Genesis 1–4*, 69.

creation care, is about bringing light into all the spheres of darkness. The writer of Genesis faithfully reveals what we know to be the human experience:

> "And I will put enmity between you and the woman, and between your offspring and hers; he will crush your head, and you will strike his heel" . . . To Adam he said, "Because you listened to your wife and ate fruit from the tree about which I commanded you, 'You must not eat from it,' Cursed is the ground because of you; through painful toil you will eat food from it all the days of your life. It will produce thorns and thistles for you and you will eat the plants of the field. By the sweat of your brow you will eat your food until you return to the ground, since from it you were taken; for dust you are and to dust you will return." (Gen 3:15, 17–19 NIV)

The fall and the idolatry of Adam and Eve has unleashed corrupted authorities and powers who, knowingly or unknowingly, are agents of this destruction against the environment and all created beings. We are part of this corrupted order. Sadly, we see the global reality of fallen stewardship every day on our television news. There is an ongoing battle against evil and darkness.

Christ has the authority to ultimately defeat evil and bring the kingdom into being (1 Cor 15:24–28). He leads the way against rebellion to destroy all the enemies of the garden, including exploitation of creation. Roy Ciampa and Brian Rosner explain this general idea would have been familiar to anyone in the Roman Empire. Just as a Roman emperor would send out his leading general to put down seditious movements to restore the emperor's authority throughout the empire, God has sent Jesus to subdue all rebellion and opposition. Jesus is to destroy all the enemies of God's kingdom, and to restore all creation to its proper submission to the Father for his glory and the good of all creation.[55]

New humanity, with a vision of the new garden, will work as stewards of Christ. We are stewards of the new Adam who goes before us. In his name, we are to fight against corruption whether it be the modern slave trade, destruction of

---

[55] Ciampa and Rosner, *First Letter.*

the environment, corruption in government, oppression of the powerless, bribery in the judiciary, or exploitation of refugees. We go against the forces with confidence as we have seen the vision of the promised land. David Bosch puts it this way, "The central theme of our missionary message is that Christ is risen, and that, secondly and consequently, the church is called to live the resurrection life in the here and now and to be a sign of contradiction against the forces of death and destruction."[56]

Intuitively the world senses the reality of the battle Christ is waging. In the most popular and influential mythical novel of recent times, *Lord of the Rings*, J. R. R. Tolkien describes a battlefield of cosmic proportions. Gandalf is locked in battle with the wicked Balrog and they both plunge into the abyss where Gandalf slays his enemy in the underworld. Gandalf rises again as Gandalf the White. This is just one of the battle scenes that portrays the mission creep of goodness over evil.

In C. S. Lewis's *The Last Battle* there is a graphic showdown between good and evil where the resurrected lion

---

56 Bosch, *Transforming Mission*, 527.

Aslan defeats his evil foe, Tashlan. Like the emperor's general or the risen Christ, Aslan then leads all of Narnia into the "True Narnia," where all the best of the promised land is to be found, beyond all one's expectations. Here again, even in a children's story, is the theme of 1 Corinthians 15.

These gripping tales have captured many a reader's mind and the screenplays have dominated our cinemas. They declare the garden is worth fighting for and there will be a new day and order. Of course, such a battle points to one who personifies evil and champions the way of darkness. Harry Potter movies have portrayed this alarmingly and powerfully. Capturing creation begins with facing and defeating the ultimate enemy. This enemy is powerfully portrayed in Genesis as the great deceiver and enemy of God.

> Now the serpent was more crafty than any of the
> wild animals the Lord God had made. He said to
> the woman, "Did God really say, 'You must not
> eat from any tree in the garden'?" The woman
> said to the serpent, "We may eat fruit from the
> trees in the garden, but God did say, 'You must
> not eat fruit from the tree that is in the middle of

173

the garden, and you must not touch it, or you will
die.'" "You will not certainly die," the serpent
said to the woman. "For God knows that when
you eat from it your eyes will be opened, and
you will be like God, knowing good and evil."
(Gen 3:1–5 NIV)

Belief in the devil is not politically correct today. However,
historian Jeffrey Russell has documented the reality of cosmic
evil and reached this conclusion:

If the Devil does exist, what is he? If the concept
has any meaning at all, he is the traditional
Prince of Darkness, a mighty person with
intelligence and will whose energies are bent on
the destruction of the cosmos and the misery of
its creatures. He is the personification of radical
evil, and he can never be irrelevant because
humans have always sought to understand and
to confront that evil. That search, that need, is
a sign that meaning is there, however obscurely
it seems to be hidden from the intellect . . . It is
easier to go to the Devil's way with hatred and
violence and indifference. But the Devil's way
not only is morally wrong; it is stupid. It will

never work; it has never worked. Violence always provokes violence; hatred everywhere provokes hatred. Daily, we are reminded that we have not yet learned this. The Devil stands like a blind man in the sun, seeing only darkness where he stands among the brilliant green fields of God's creation. We have thought the Devil's way long enough. It is time for a new way of thinking.[57]

The glorious message is, as Paul declares in the Scripture above, that in the resurrected Christ the battle is eventually won. All creation is again good. To be a follower of the resurrected Jesus, as stewards, is to be engaged in his creation battles and assured, even in martyrdom, of the certainty of kingdom victory and new life in Narnia.

Stewardship in the New Garden —Third Movement

There is a visionary portrayal of the new garden in Revelation 21–22, where the apostle John sees the holy city, the new Jerusalem,

---

57 Russell, *Prince of Darkness*, 276–77.

175

coming down out of heaven to earth. In these chapters, we have images that connect with those of the opening two chapters of the Bible: rivers, trees, and light. Eternity is not spent robed in white playing the harp on some proverbial distant cloud; it is lived as whole people on a restored earth. Revelation 22:1–5 sets our sights on such a hope. It is transformative:

> Then the angel showed me the river of the water
> of life, as clear as crystal, flowing from the
> throne of God and of the Lamb down the middle
> of the great street of the city. On each side of
> the river stood the tree of life, bearing twelve
> crops of fruit, yielding its fruit every month.
> And the leaves of the tree are for the healing of
> the nations. No longer, will there be any curse.
> The throne of God and of the Lamb will be in
> the city, and his servants will serve him. They
> will see his face, and his name will be on their
> foreheads. There will be no more night. They
> will not need the light of a lamp or the light of
> the sun, for the Lord God will give them light.
> And they will reign for ever and ever.

As we have discussed in chapter 1 and throughout this book there is a deep connection between this present creation and the re-created world to come. Theologian Hoekema explains it this way:

> There will be a continuity as well as discontinuity between this age and the next, and between this earth and the new earth. This point is extremely important. As citizens of God's kingdom, we may not just write off the present earth as a total loss, or rejoice in its deterioration. We must indeed be working for a better world now. Our efforts to be bringing the kingdom of Christ into fuller manifestation are of eternal significance. Our Christian life today, our struggles against sin—both individual and institutional—our mission work . . . have value not only for this world but even for the world to come.[58]

God will not let go of this world as he plans its renewal. Those who have this vision and understanding will honor Jesus's prayer, "Your kingdom come, your will be done on earth as it

---

58 Hoekema, *Bible and the Future*, 287.

is in heaven" (Matt 6:10). Therefore, we should connect with our planet now and show Godly care for it in our environmental stewardship. This is the Father's world and his children are to love and look after his created order of trees, rivers, mountains, and oceans. We are to seek to enhance and not diminish our environment as we "rule" and "subdue" for his glory and for the benefit of those who come after us.

Apart from our care for the environment, elsewhere I have set out what the Bible, and in particular the Prophets, portray the new garden to be. It is of the same character as the first, only magnified. This is the coming kingdom of Christ which we aspire to now and with God's Spirit we work for:

- God's rule will be just, in welcome contrast to the injustice and corruption, that sometimes overwhelms us. We will know justice and integrity of government (Isa 11:5; Jer 23).

- God's rule will be peaceful, in contrast to the wars and rumors of wars that surround us. We will live in peace and security (Mic 4; Isa 2:2–4). Jesus is to be known as the Prince of Peace (Isa 9:6).

- God's rule will be everlasting, in contrast to the transience of the nations, which rise and fall (Mic 4; Isa 9:7).

- God's rule will be universally effective, in contrast to the shortcomings of our best efforts such as the United Nations (Rev 21:22–26). Isaiah the prophet declared, "The LORD Almighty will prepare a feast of rich food for all people, a banquet of aged wine— the best of meats and the finest of wines . . . he will destroy the shroud that enfolds all peoples, the sheet that covers all nations" (Isa 25:6–7).

- God's rule will be a cause of worship and rejoicing (Isa 12; Rev 4–5). Eugene Peterson, in his version of Psalm 84 in the contemporary translation *The Message*, lifts us up by saying that one day spent in the Lord's house "beats thousands spent on Greek island beaches."

- God's rule will eliminate pain and suffering. "'He will wipe every tear from their eyes. There will be

179

no more death' or mourning or crying or pain, for the old order of things has passed away" (Rev 21:4).[59] Stewardship in the garden extends to the animal kingdom. C. S. Lewis in *The Last Battle* lets the children meet their animals in the new garden, for "no good thing is ever lost." Jesus himself said, "Are not two sparrows sold for a penny? Yet not one of them will fall to the ground apart from the will of your Father" (Matt 10:29 BSB). And remember the last day's picture of Isaiah the prophet where the wolf and the lamb lie down together. Yes indeed, they praise their creator (Ps 148).

Followers of Jesus have been at the forefront of stewardship to animals. Social justice advocates for the dignity of all humanity, such as William Wilberforce, were instrumental in establishing the RSPCA. The great Baptist evangelist and preacher C. H. Spurgeon championed stewardship towards animals:

Treat all creatures kindly, then, as far as you can, for the great Creator's sake. I would not have a sparrow needlessly killed, nor even a worm trod on that might be spared. My Lord and Master

---

59 Clifford and Johnson, *Riding the Rollercoaster,* 108–9.

made them all—and when I look at them, I see traces of His wonderful wisdom and power! And when I see how bountifully He provides for them, I note the tokens of His goodness and care. He opens His hands and satisfies the desire of every living thing! There is not a little bird that picks up a seed by the roadside that was not created by Christ and for Him! And, perhaps, answers its end better than some of you who lift your brows to yonder Heaven only to defy your Maker! There is not an animal upon the common, nor a lion in the forest, nor a fish in the sea, nor a fowl in the air that was not made by Him—and that does not in some way promote His glory![60]

Living in the New Garden —Fourth Movement

Poet John Donne poignantly penned, "No man is an island unto himself." Creation care that emphasizes Christian stewardship

---

60 Spurgeon, Sermon 3180, 31. All references to his sermons derive from the Christian Classics Ethereal Library at www.ccel.org/ccel/spurgeon.

is one of partnership, followers of the way together making a difference whilst awaiting the final restoration through Christ's return. Psalms 96, 98 and 148 declare that the trees, sun, seas, rivers, mountains, wind, stars, and birds join in the dance of giving praise to God. This is a transformative vision. Romans 8:28 announces that the whole of creation groans and waits for this healing of the earth. We are interconnected with the environment, in a global village seeking the restoration. This is captured in a forgotten adaption of Wesley's most popular Christmas hymn, "Hark the Herald Angels Sing."[61]

Joyful, all ye nations rise,

Join the triumph of the skies;

Universal nature say:

"Christ the Lord is born today"

Now display thy saving power,

Ruined nature now restore,

---

61 See original text for "Hymn for Christmas Day," 1739.

Now in mystic union join

Thine to ours and ours to thine.

Our stewardships for the environment can take many forms. In the particular transactions we undertake we must keep the transformative vision before us. Otherwise we will see this as simply work rather than the vision and power of the risen Christ, through the Holy Spirit, working in us. Our transactions may be as basic as monitoring our use of electricity and fuel, the support of free-range chickens, political engagement on environmental issues, and so on. Irrespective of our political allegiances, we must be involved as followers of Jesus who are endowed with strong hope. After all, as Genesis 1 reminds us, we are ourselves created from dust!

The transformative vision and the transactional action of Micah Challenge can assist us here. For a five-year period, from 2010 to 2015, thousands of Christians gathered across the planet in their respective nation's capital, to advocate on behalf of Micah Challenge for the Millennium Development Goals. The eight goals were to eradicate extreme poverty and hunger, achieve universal primary education, promote gender equality and empower women, reduce child mortality, improve maternal health, combat HIV/AIDS, malaria and other diseases, ensure environment sustainability, and develop a global partnership for development. The gatherings were representative of all ages, ethnic backgrounds, and denominational links. The Millennium Development Goals were agreed to by the United Nations and were appropriately adapted by people of goodwill. Not all the MDGs were met but there was certainly progresses made, and on many indicators, faster than any time since such records have been kept. The keeping of data and breaking down of effectiveness region by region is complex but those who invested in this creation stewardship have made a difference. For example, the aim was to halve the proportion of people living in extreme poverty (46.7%) as well as halving the portion of hungry people (18.6%). Those targets, with the commitment of governments, care agencies, churches, and people of goodwill, appear to have been met or substantially met. With respect to ensuring that all

children can complete primary school the percentage of 81.9%
has now increased into the ninetieth percentile.[62]

New transactions consistent with the transformative
vision of the new garden are needed to build on the Millennium
Development Goals. Transactions such as the Sustainable
Development Goals are being considered by many Christian
agencies. They include a sustainable/environmental agenda and
a development/anti-poverty perspective. There are goals such as:

poverty eradication, changing unsustainable and
promoting sustainable patterns of consumption
and production and protecting and managing
the natural resource base of economic and social
development . . . [63]

Another of the goals addresses the environment:

Climate change calls for the widest possible
cooperation by all countries and their
participation in an effective and appropriate
international response, with a view to

62 Harris and Provost, "Millennium Development Goals."

63 United Nations, "Open Working Group Proposal."

accelerating the reduction of global greenhouse

gas emissions.[64]

Another practical way one can make a difference here comes

from the annuals of the Micah Challenge. It is estimated that

$160 billion in tax is robbed from developing nations annually,

more than the $120 billion they receive in foreign aid. Developed

countries such as America, England, and Australia can advance

the push on multinationals to ensure they publicly report their

operations and activities in every country they operate. At

the 2014 G20 Summit in Brisbane, global tax avoidance was

identified by the national leaders as being a key issue for their

agenda. With right reporting and payment of appropriate taxes

by corporations in developing countries, essential services

such as health, education, infrastructure, and water can be

enhanced. With this amended tax revenue being made available

it is estimated that around 350,000 children could be saved

from death through poverty every year. The way of Jesus calls

multinational executives and shareholders to look at ways they

can constructively transform current tax practice.

---

64 United Nations, "Open Working Group Proposal."

Are all these transformational goals just a "bucket list" of unobtainable targets? In our complex world, where there are no easy solutions, it may appear so at times. That is why the apparent immensity of the targets must not overtake the transformative vision. Step by step, with the risen Lord by our side, those who bear the mark of the new Adam will in their own way, and together, go about garden restoration. Tom Wright is inspirational in his summation:

> With the resurrection of Jesus God's new world has begun; in other words, his being raised from the dead is the start, the paradigm case, the foundation, the beginning, of that great setting-right which God will do for the whole cosmos at the end. The risen body of Jesus is the one bit of the physical universe that has already been "set right." Jesus is therefore the one through whom everything else will be "set right."[65]

That is the vision for the followers of the way of Jesus. It inspires our living in the garden as stewards of God's glory.

---

65 Wright, *Acts for Everyone*, 93.

CHAPTER 8:

OUR HUNGER FOR THE GARDEN

We know that the whole creation has been groaning as in the pains of childbirth right up to the present time. (Rom 8:22 NIV)

We, as planetary citizens, are creating a new quality of life for the new millennium! . . . The love of power will be replaced by the power of love! . . . The military will revert to peace-time activities! . . . Governments will recognise their

true role of serving the people and the living planet! . . . We will develop a right relationship between male and female . . . we will eradicate violence in thought, word and deed . . . we will celebrate the birth of the new earth.
O'le-an, New Millennium Proclamation

I began to read American Indian myths, and it wasn't long before I found the same motifs in the American Indian stories that I was being taught by the nuns at school.[66]

When speaking on motifs in our society that point to the resurrection, we often begin with the Harry Potter analogy. It goes like this: Who am I? My birth was predicted, I have both extraordinary (wizard) and ordinary (Muggle) strengths and credentials, I gathered together a motley group of disciples, I fought the ultimate evil one and his gross serpent, I descended into the underworld, I placed my faith in the Father (Dumbledore) and I ascended in triumph. The reaction of the audience is

---

66 Campbell and Moyers, *Power of Myth*, 10.

understandably to answer Jesus. When we respond, "Harry Potter" there is a kind of aha moment!

This is the Harry Potter story that projected its creator, J. K. Rowling, into the world's most successful storyteller. It was not enough for Harry to die; it needed a happy ending. A new day inaugurated by Potter's "death" and victory, an epic tale of biblical proportions. It is a story, because of its dark side, that has not thrilled some concerned readers, but the biblical imagery is most evident.

Before Harry Potter

J. K. Rowling did not invent her story outline. She was well versed in the writings of J. R. R. Tolkien and C. S. Lewis before she wrote. Harry Potter is a Christ-type figure somewhat in line with Christlike characters found in the novels of Tolkien and Lewis.[67]

In Tolkien's *Lord of the Rings* the grey wizard Gandalf dies in a battle with the evil Balrog to save his companions and

---

67 Garrett, *One Fine Potion.*

190

then rises as the glorious white wizard. In Lewis's *The Lion, The Witch and the Wardrobe*, Aslan the lion dies for the sins of the boy. In The *Last Battle* all the inhabitants of Narnia are resurrected and they meet the resurrected Aslan in a day of judgment.

The books written by Tolkien, Lewis, and Rowling are extraordinarily successful and their stories have touched and inspired many. At the heart of the same lies, what Tolkien tagged "Eucatastrophies." They are happy event situations as characters are rescued from perilous ones. Tolkien insisted:

> the gospels contain . . . a story of a larger kind
> which embraces all the essence of fairy stories . .
> . The birth of Christ is the eucatastrophe of man's
> history. The resurrection is the eucatastrophe of
> the story of the incarnation. This story begins
> and ends in joy. It has pre-eminently the "inner
> consistency of reality." There is no tale ever told
> that men would rather find was true, and none
> which so many sceptical men have accepted as
> true on its own merits. For the art of it has the
> supremely convincing tone of primary art, that

is, of creation. To reject it leads either to sadness
or to wrath.[68]

C. S. Lewis also had a positive view of how the story of Jesus
fulfills our deep longings, found even in pagan mythology. The
following quotation not only explains how Lewis, who as a non-
Christian scholar had delved into pagan mythology, personally
came to understand the truth of Christianity but the breadth of
its revelation.

> The heart of Christianity is a myth which
> is also a fact . . . We must not be ashamed of
> the mythical radiance resting on our theology.
> We must not be nervous about "parallels" and
> "Pagan Christs": they ought to be there—it
> would be a stumbling block if they weren't.
> We must not, in false spirituality, withhold our
> imaginative welcome. If God chooses to be
> mythopoeic—and is not the sky itself a myth?—
> shall we refuse to be mythopathic? For this is the
> marriage of heaven and earth: Perfect Myth and

68 Tolkein, "On Fairy Stories," 83–84.

Perfect Fact: claiming not only our love and our
obedience, but also our wonder and delight.[69]

This resurrection longing, found in the writing of Rowling,
Tolkien, and Lewis, is twofold. It's for one who would come
and lead us in battle between good and evil into the new day,
and it's that we might also share in the defeat of death through
the breadth of resurrection life. Sociologist Peter Berger in his
seminal book A *Rumour of Angels* investigated our common
hope for a new day, "deathlessness." He concluded:

> Our "no!" to death—be it the frantic fear of
> our own annihilation, in moral outrage at the
> death of a loved other, or in death-defying acts
> of courage and self-sacrifice—appears to be an
> intrinsic constituent of our being. There seems
> to be a death-refusing hope at the very core
> of our humanitas . . . In a world where we are
> surrounded by death on all sides, we continue to
> be a being who says "no!" to death—and through
> this "no!" is brought faith in another world.[70]

---

69 Lewis, *God in the Dock*, 66–67.

70 Berger, *Rumor of Angels*, x.

More Surprising Signs

This twofold dimension is found in other surprising places. The tarot card deck is one of the major tools for guidance for today's New Spirituality seeker. As mentioned in a previous chapter, the New Spirituality devotee or dabbler is singly defined as one who is eclectic in their spiritual journey and begins with a self-spirituality that is the desire to be the best person they can possibly be. The transformative search in this movement occurs outside the church and traditional religious services. It often incorporates a little bit of Buddhist meditation, Taoism wisdom, Feng Shui practices, Christian principles, and Hindu thought. They follow a mantra such as "I'm spiritual but not religious." New Spirituality is one of the fastest growing spiritual movements in the Western world. Its spiritual heroes and guides are numerous but certainly include Oprah, Deepak Chopra, Wayne Dyer, and Elizabeth Gilbert (*Eat, Pray, Love*). Those exploring and experimenting New Spirituality include our next-door neighbor, business partner, and soccer mum. It is part of our mainstream life today.

I have explained elsewhere that the tarot cards are full of biblical imagery, especially from the book of Revelation. They are like the PowerPoint of the Renaissance. It was probably in the nineteenth century that these cards started to be used for prediction. The cards progressively reveal Adam and Eve, in an idealistic state in the garden (lovers card), the fall with Adam and Eve now in chains and lorded over by the devil on his throne (devil card), and restoration as seen through resurrection from the grave (judgment card). The joker card is key to this restoration and the popular authority on mythologies, Joseph Campbell, indicates the joker is the dying and rising sun god found in most pagan religions. The cards point to the resurrection of Jesus and resurrection living in a re-created world, a world that encapsulates harmony, strength, and wisdom (chariot card). In a one-to-one, or group setting, the biblical narrative from Genesis to Revelation can be simply explained from this deck of cards.[71]

Vampire spirituality is the new emerging folk religion in North American, Europe, and Australia.[72] Classical tales

---

71 Drane et al., *Beyond Prediction.*

72 Hume, "Liminal Beings," 3–16; Keyworth, "Socio-Religious Beliefs."

about vampires, and other undead creatures such as werewolves and zombies, have captured a large readership. Vampires and werewolves feed on the blood of the living in a way that parodies the death of Christ and his shedding his blood. Stories like *The Vampire* and *Frankenstein* pick up the loss of being in the image of God (*imago Dei*) that many experienced in the harshness of the Industrial Revolution. Some characters seek to cheat death through the sucking of blood. Others, like the Frankenstein monster, convey the bankruptcy of seeking immortality in the flesh through earthly, not heavenly, resurrection.

Newer vampire stories such as *Twilight* have a strong romantic flavor. There is a theme of redeeming the bad guys as well as the search for acceptance and love. How can we be restored to the ideal of the first garden? Anne Rice, author of *Interview with the Vampire*, commented on the fascination with vampires:

> Since the vampire starts out as a human being, it's quite natural to explore the idea of his wanting redemption, or to put an end to his cursed existence of drinking human blood. In

other words, the myth is very compatible with Christian ideas and can obviously be developed well in that direction.[73]

The very popular film trilogy *The Matrix* is another indicator of common connections to the resurrection and the hope it entails. Although the plotline of the trilogy is complex and involves a variety of philosophical perspectives, there is a clear resurrection theme. In the first film Neo is shot dead and he surprised all by his rising from the dead. It is a story with messianic proportions. In the second film, *Matrix Reloaded*, it's Neo who resurrects Trinity after she is fatally wounded.[74]

Much has been written about the connection between religious themes and Dr Who. This globally loved fictional character was an inspiration for the virtual world of *The Matrix*. A recurring thread throughout the series is this Time Lord's regeneration. Since 2005, each time his resurrection is portrayed the Doctor stands in a crucifixion pose as his body dissolves and a new one appears out of blinding light. In every resurrection

---

73 Evans, "Power in the Blood," 38.

74 *Matrix Reloaded* (Warner Bros, 2003).

the Doctor goes through a physical transformation; he is the same man but has a different appearance.[75] This is a handy way to move from one actor to another playing the central character. Yet within this transformation motif there is an echo of what we considered in our first chapter. When Mary Magdalene first met the risen Christ, the new gardener, she did not recognize him. Jesus arose the same but, to the naked eye, was also at times different in his resurrection body. Barry Letts was for some time the producer of Dr Who and he indicated we should expect to find religious parables in the series as it deals with "the fight between good and evil" and "will have some Christian themes as a backdrop."[76]

It is our belief that Genesis 1–2 is a universal "story" of creation and humanity.

In these chapters, there is no mention of Israel or Jerusalem. These chapters do not seek to speak to a particular tribe, culture, or nation. It is a factual account of how God is the creator and the role and place of all people, irrespective

---

75 Johnson, "Here We Go Again."

76 Barry Letts interviewed in Wynne-Jones, "The Church Is Ailing."

of race, in his garden. It is a story that because of the fall we suppress and distort as we seek redemption and restoration. Yet it is a story that still bubbles away within all of us and creative geniuses like Tolkien stir certain aspects of the narrative that lies dormant within.

Acts 17 and the Garden

This "stirring" is the approach of the apostle Paul as found in Acts 17 from verse 16:

> While Paul was waiting for them in Athens, he was greatly distressed to see that the city was full of idols. So he reasoned in the synagogue with both Jews and God-fearing Greeks, as well as in the marketplace day by day with those who happened to be there. A group of Epicurean and Stoic philosophers began to debate with him. Some of them asked, "What is this babbler trying to say?" Others remarked, "He seems to be advocating foreign gods." They said this because Paul was preaching the good news about Jesus and the resurrection. Then they took him

199

and brought him to a meeting of the Areopagus, where they said to him, "May we know what this new teaching is that you are presenting? You are bringing some strange ideas to our ears, and we would like to know what they mean." (All the Athenians and the foreigners who lived there spent their time doing nothing but talking about and listening to the latest ideas.)

Paul then stood up in the meeting of the Areopagus and said: "People of Athens! I see that in every way you are very religious. For as I walked around and looked carefully at your objects of worship, I even found an altar with this inscription: TO AN UNKNOWN GOD. So you are ignorant of the very thing you worship— and this is what I am going to proclaim to you.

"The God who made the world and everything in it is the Lord of heaven and earth and does not live in temples built by human hands. And he is not served by human hands, as if he needed anything. Rather, he himself gives everyone life and breath and everything else. From one man he made all the nations, that they should inhabit the whole earth; and he marked out their appointed times in history and the boundaries of their lands. God did this so that they would seek him and perhaps reach out for him and find him, though he is not far from any one of us. 'For in him we live and move and have our being.' As some of your own poets have said, 'We are his offspring.'

"Therefore since we are God's offspring, we should not think that the divine being is like gold or silver or stone—an image made by human design and skill. In the past God overlooked such ignorance, but now he commands all people everywhere to repent. For he has set a day when he will judge the world with justice by the man he has appointed. He has given proof of this to everyone by raising him from the dead."

When they heard about the resurrection of the dead, some of them sneered, but others said, "We want to hear you again on this subject."
(Acts 17:16–33 NIV)

In this great missionary passage, Paul stands before the Areopagus and shares the biblical story. In Paul's day, this council appeared to still have some religious and civil oversight. As they were biblically illiterate, he does not open the Old Testament Scriptures, as he did in the synagogues (Acts 17:1–4). In his, and Peter's, speeches before Jewish audiences the concentration was on Israel's history and that Jesus was the fulfillment of Old Testament prophecy (Acts 2:25–38; 13:16–41). Rather here, Paul presents a message from the general revelation of God that is available to all. His talk is consistent with a biblical plotline. It is consistent with the brief speech he gave at Lystra, also a non-Jewish crowd (Acts 14:14–16). Before the Areopagus he outlines that God created the world, gave mortals breath, that we all come from one ancestor, and that God is not far from all of us. He challenges other ancient creation stories from the Babylonian world. As is the case in Genesis 1–2, Paul states there is only one God, not a plethora of gods, who is preeminent, not created, and that the world does not come into being through a cosmic battle with anything. Nor are the sun, moon, and planets to be worshipped. This is the "unknown" God, worthy of praise, who is sovereign over all. Paul quotes their poets, "For we too are his offering," revealing that the true biblical account is a narrative that threads through the history of humanity.

Paul then outlines our rejection of God's purposes and that Christ, who is the climax and verification of the story, is the way back to a relationship with him. He centers on the resurrection, mentioning it three times (17:18, 31, 32). As Alister McGrath observes:

> In the end, the debate with the New Age (New Spirituality) movement will not be won through philosophy, but through the proclamation of Christ . . . Paul's Areopagus sermon sets before us a crisp, concise, and convincing approach, ideally suited to the New Age challenge— both in terms of the movement's ideas, and the opportunities available for confronting it. As for the Athenians, the resurrection of Christ may hold the key to engagement with New Agers.[77]

Paul speaks of the resurrection of the dead as he develops his resurrection theology (v. 32). As previously mentioned, some of his listeners scoffed but some are drawn to his words. The scoffing was not over Jesus's resurrection as such, as the Greeks in their myths explored the idea of a deity coming back from the

---

77 McGrath, *Springboard for Faith*, 78.

dead, even if it was not in any historical sense. They were more likely scoffing at the suggestion that mortals could be caught up in a resurrection life. Paul stirred up the creation story and the search for redemption that lay within their own experience.

R. C. Sproul can assist us in our understanding here. He holds that our response to the general knowledge of God has three basic stages: trauma, repression, and substitution. Like Adam and Eve, God's self-revelation is awesome and threatens our own autonomy (trauma). So, we repress it and substitute it for other gods like the Athenians did. However, this process of denial does not obliterate the knowledge of the universal story that lurks within our own subconscious.[78] It's this distorted common story that still lives on that Tolkien, Lewis, and others draw us to. However, it is in the factual story of the resurrection of Jesus alone that we find real redemption, true meaning, and a home in the re-created garden.

---

78 Sproul, *If There is a God*, 56–80.

Nature Speaks

Throughout Scripture, it is declared that nature bears the handiwork of God and serves his purpose. King David sung "the heavens declare the glory of God; the skies proclaim the works of his hands. Day after day they pour forth speech; night after night they reveal knowledge" (Psalm 19:1–2). We are touched by the fact that the rainbow and a star configuration respectively proclaim God's grace over a flood-judged creation and that the culmination of that grace is the birth of his son, Jesus (Gen 9:8–16, Matt 2:1–2).

The apostle Paul poignantly revealed that although nature speaks of God and his ways it is still fallen. He declared, "We know that the whole creation has been groaning as in the pains of childbirth right up to the present time" (Rom 8:23). A few verses earlier Paul speaks of creation being "subjected to frustration" but it now waits in eager expectation for "liberation from its bondage to decay."

Leon McKenzie explains the state of nature this way. He argues that, although the garden is fallen, it still in its very heart cries out for renewal and that God has put resurrection analogies in the very structures of creation. He refers to the ancient pagan myths of the sun dying and rising, our own experiences of sleep and wakefulness as examples.[79] Then there is ageing life that comes to nature itself through death at autumn and re-creation at spring. And, one could add, doesn't the caterpillar DNA include the capacity to change into a butterfly? A further illustration is something I noticed a few years ago when driving through a national park on the edge of a city that had recently been devastated by a major forest fire. The plants and trees had begun regenerating and the park rangers had erected roadside signs declaring, "The Royal National Park lives again!" These analogies, from the bushfire to the caterpillar, point to the fact that in nature itself there are signs of fallenness, and a longing for re-creation through death and resurrection. In the true "royal," Jesus, we have the promise of new life!

This nature theme is developed by early church fathers such as Clement of Rome. He, relying on Paul, stressed that Jesus's

---

79 McKenzie, *Pagan Resurrection Myths.*

resurrection was the firstfruits of the harvest (1 Cor 15:20) and that this seed imagery gives birth to all sorts of natural world analogies. Of such writings and thoughts, it is said,

> The metaphors for resurrection in this early literature are naturalistic images that stress return or repetition: the cycle of the seasons, the flowering of trees and shrubs, the coming of dawn after darkness, the fertility of seeds . . . The point of the metaphors is to emphasize God's power and the goodness of the creation. If the Lord can bring spring after winter . . . he can bring back men and women who sleep in the grave.[80]

The hymn "How Great Thou Art" is based on a Swedish poem written by Carl Boberg. The melody is a Swedish folk song, and it was popularized by George Beverly Shea in the Billy Graham crusades. It, together with Amazing Grace, is among the most popular and well-sung hymns of today. It appeals to churchgoers and non-church goers alike. Proof of this is Elvis Presley winning a Grammy for his rendition. Why so popular?

---

80 Bynum, *Resurrection of the Body*, 24–26.

Perhaps the answer lies in the fact that the first two verses connect us all to the wonder of God's creation. This is the world we know, but yet long for:

Lord my God! When I in awesome wonder

Consider all the works thy hand hath made

Refrain:

Then sings my soul, my Saviour God, to Thee,

How great Thou art, how great Thou art!

Gloriously Lewis rightly summarizes, "nature is only the image, the symbol; but it is the symbol Scripture invites me to use. We are summoned to pass in and through nature, beyond her, into that splendor in which she fully reflects."[81]

---

81 Lewis, "Weight of Glory," 8.

Are People Open?

It is often claimed that we live in a postmodern world that rejects metanarratives, or if you will, worldview stories. People are suspicious of those who claim to have an answer "to life, the universe and everything." Whilst it is fair to say people are cautious of those who spruik ultimate answers, it does not mean there is a total aversion to metanarratives. Rather, there is a strong aversion to those whose worldview is disempowering or who argue a case with arrogance and lack of respect. As we have seen, the resurrection life is not disempowering but liberation and quality for all. Return to the garden through resurrection is restoration of all that is good. The openness to a common story today is seen in the reels of Hollywood. George Lucas, director of the Star Wars trilogy offered, "I consciously set out to re-create myths and the classic mythological motifs. I wanted to use these motifs to deal with issues that exist today. The more research I did, the more I realized that the issues are the same that existed 3,000 years ago."[82]

Another aspect is that postmodern spirituality today, that is the New Spirituality mentioned earlier, places a strong emphasis on universal myth. New Spirituality in its search clearly shows an appreciation of common inner life and a common human condition. As mentioned in a previous chapter, I am connected to a ministry that is called The Community of Hope, which sets up booths in MindBodySpirit festivals. There the modern-day seeker openly hears the universal story of the tarot cards, the movies, Tolkien, and Lewis. Their own spiritual journey places a strong emphasis on myth. As academic Robert Ellwood comments, although modern spiritualties may appear diverse, they are "in effect, one message, based on the psychic unity of humanity, and proclaimed intrapsychic path to salvation."[83] There is a universal longing for return to the good life of the garden via the resurrected one. This is evidenced in Neville Drury's tale of four occult shamans from different

---

82 Moyers, "Interview with George Lucas."

83 Ellwood, *Politics of Myth*, 174.

corners of the globe who come together at the mythic center of the world to witness a healing of the earth. The healing is based on a common story handed down from the "ancient ones."[84]

Sadly, as George Miller, the creator of the Babe movies, and director of the Mad Max trilogies commented, the cinema storytellers have become the new priests. They're doing a lot of the work of our religious institutions, which have so concretized the metaphors in their stories, taken so much of the poetry, mystery, and mysticism out of religious belief, that people look for other places to question their spirituality.[85] It is there, and not the church, that many turn to for the story of redemption and hope.

Missional Models
The Resurrection

We have sought to illustrate the common connections to the resurrection theme and the restored garden through books,

84 Drury, *Shaman's Quest*, 188.

85 George Miller quoted in Hawley, "The Hero's Journey," 57.

movies, nature, and the like. Paradise lost is paradise regained! This is creation hope and the resurrection of Jesus found in the marketplace, beyond the walls of the church. It's a biblical link that Paul superbly models in his talk to the Areopagus. We should live our lives with our eyes wide open to God's revelation. It should draw us to awesome wonder, reflection, and praise in our own lives: "How Great Thou Art"! It reminds us of what we have been created for and opens doors for conversations with others about the ultimate purpose for God's creation and us.[86]

The "Play of Life"

Throughout this chapter, we have sought to outline various ministry models of how we can illustrate our cultural connections with the creation and the resurrection story. Here are two more that God has used to touch people's lives.

The "Play of Life" demonstrates how the re-creation in Christ truly is empowering and touches all aspects of life in the garden. It is an interactive model devised by Argentinean

---

86 For more examples see Clifford and Johnson, *Cross is Not Enough*, 91–109.

Christian Carlos Raimundo. We have witnessed its healing potential when it was adopted by a government agency to support abused women in Mexico City and its touching the personal lives of seekers at a MindBodySpirit festival. We have also witnessed it minister to followers of Jesus in a counseling environment. It connects God's redemptive purpose to all.

Simply, it begins with a brief one-to-one chat about problems a person may be experiencing. The person is then invited to create a sculpture on a board of how they feel using small plastic figures that represent their relationships with their partner, family, friends, at the workplace, and with God. After further dialogue, the person is encouraged to create a positive sculpture of how they would prefer their situation to be in all of these areas. The sculptures represent a before and after portrait. They are then asked to consider how change can occur so with God's strength they can move to the after portrait. During this time of reflection, there may be a massage to allow the calming of the body and emotions as well as prayer in the name of the risen Jesus for a return in their lives to the order and delights of the garden.

213

The "Play of Life" embodies the theology of the resurrection with forgiveness, wholeness, and newness of life, which reaches into family, work, play, and creation spheres. We have witnessed the incredible response to this simple ministry aid. For example, in festivals it is not uncommon for the public to vote this the "booth of the festival."

Wicca/Trunk or Treat

It greatly distresses us (Acts 17:16) that many young women, in particular, are attracted to this neo-pagan spirituality. It is a modern nature-based form of spirituality that takes many forms, but it is often connected to Gaia, the mother goddess, which we considered in the chapter on creation care. Understandably, Christians are concerned about its relationship to Western witchcraft and that needs to be taken seriously. However, it also strongly relates to the universal story we have been considering. As this movement "surges" through Western world schools and universities, it is vital that we explain the salvation connections. The Wiccan Wheel of the Year includes an eight-episode story that coincides with changes in the seasons and equinoxes. As the story unfolds, there is a virginal goddess, who carries the child of promise, and a dying and rising god myth. As the New Testament gospels reveal, the virgin will be with child and the child will die, be buried, and rise again.[87]

We have witnessed how the connection with Wicca can be shared with youth groups and the like and bring people out of darkness to the empowering light of the risen Christ. As Jim's church in their "Trunk or Treat" outreach turn Halloween from a festival bowing before witches and goblins to one showing their defeat in the risen Christ, so the Wiccan wheel is transformed. However, in all this discipleship endeavor, the cross and resurrection of Jesus must be primary, and like Paul in Acts 17 the dangers and deceptions of the "unknown gods" must be taken seriously and spoken of.

---

87 Johnson and Smulo, "Wiccan and Mother Goddess Devotees."

Longing

People long for restoration to the garden; to be living in the light of the second Adam, the new gardener. The Bible fully reveals what culture and nature dimly reveal. The garden and the message of Jesus risen is all around us! Missional opportunities focused on the fourth movement, from the old to the new garden, abound.

Resurrection Sunday

A glorious unveiling, lightning, presence,
a tearing, releasing, breathless running.
News that exploded like soul searing fission,
for Jerusalem, Empire, Age, a tired Earth.
But a touching, a healing, a balm like no other,
the bunting of grace in the shards of cruelty,
the banner of joy for the grimace of sadness.[88]

---

88 Stiles, *Resurrection Sunday.*

CONCLUSION

I want to know Christ—yes, to know the power of his resurrection and participation in his sufferings, becoming like him in his death, and so, somehow, attaining to the resurrection from the dead. Not that I have already obtained all this, or have already arrived at my goal, but I press on to take hold of that for which Christ Jesus took hold of me. (Phil 3:10–12 NIV)

The most dangerous idea in human history and philosophy remains the belief that Jesus Christ was the Son of God and rose from the dead and that is the most dangerous idea you will ever

*encounter . . . Because it alters the whole of
human behaviour and all our responsibilities.
It turns the universe from a meaningless chaos
into a designed place in which there is justice
and there is hope and, therefore, we all have a
duty to discover the nature of that justice and
work towards that hope. It alters us all. If we
reject it, it alters us all as well. It is incredibly
dangerous. It's why so many people turn against
it. (Former atheist Peter Hitchens, brother of
Christopher Hitchens.)* [89]

The Life of Discipleship: To reimagine what God has called us to be

Through our journey from the first garden to the new garden
of the risen Christ, we have discovered that discipleship is
transformational. It's understanding how God created us to be
(Genesis 1 and 2), what was lost through the fall (Genesis 3), what

89 Q & A during the "Festival of Dangerous Ideas," 2013. See https://phillipjensen.com/resources/the-most-dangerous-idea/.

is recaptured in the resurrection of Jesus, and rising to that life. It is a symphony of four movements, a call to follow Christ from the cross to a new creation. For our transformed resurrection discipleship living we have discovered seven steps/habits:

Step 1: Overcoming shame

Step 2: Rediscovering work

Step 3: Embracing wholeness and wellness

Step 4: Standing for love and marriage

Step 5: Reclaiming rest and the Sabbath

Step 6: Committing to stewardship and creation care

Step 7: Sharing the gospel and being missional

Step 8: Loving God, loving others

In our resurrection life these seven steps are dependent on rediscovering the vertical and horizontal life of the garden. In the first garden, Adam and Eve were right with God and right with each other. That is why Jesus proclaimed the law to be summed up by "Love the Lord your God with all your heart and with your soul and with all your mind . . . and love your neighbour as yourself" (Luke 10:35–37). The ultimate test that

219

we are right with God is not what church we attend, or what songs we sing, or groups we join, but that we love one another. Our horizontal relationships are evidence of the truth and strength of our vertical relationship with God. That is the ultimate mantra of resurrection living; love God, love your neighbour. That is the life of the first garden and the second garden.

What we see in Genesis is the breakdown of this truth. The first two sins of the Bible are Adam and Eve out of kilter with God (Genesis 3), and then humanity is out of kilter with each other (Genesis 4—brother kills brother). The seven steps flow from connection with God and love of each other.

To be right with God is to be friends with God, through trust in the life, death, and resurrection of Jesus. The apostle Paul shares:

> For what I received I passed on to you as of first importance: that Christ died for our sins according to the Scriptures, that he was buried, that he was raised on the third day according to the Scriptures, and that he appeared to Cephas (Peter), and then to the Twelve. (1 Cor 15:3–5 NIV)

This passage is trustworthy. It is the same message the apostles shared, as recorded in the preaching accounts in the book of Acts. Even hardened skeptics agree it was written by Paul, and there is no doubt that as we read it, is how the early church received it. In fact, it was a creedal statement of the first Christians. In unison with Jesus's followers throughout the ages we declare these words. The gospel is more than this, but must at least embrace these simple truths, that this Christ event is the foundation for our relationship with God and return to the "garden."

To be right with our neighbor is to ensure there is no nonperson status that calls us to treat all people irrespective of race, gender, economic status, and culture background with human dignity and human worth.

Nonperson status is rampant in Genesis. Genesis is not just a story of faithfulness and covenant, and scholars often fail to recognize that one of the themes in Genesis 12–50 is the actual outworking of the fall (Gen 1–3). The central characters (Abraham, Isaac, and Sarah) at times protect themselves out of sheer self-interest and treat spouses, children, significant others,

221

and other ethnic groups as nonpersons. Abraham, to protect himself, passes his wife Sarah off as his sister (Gen 12:10–20). This exposes her to an adulterous situation with Pharaoh, and God and Pharaoh both become outraged. Isaac does the same to his wife later in Genesis (26:6–11). And Sarah follows suit by treating her maidservant Hagar disgracefully (Gen 16; 21:8–21). Hagar, through no fault of her own, bears a child to Abraham, but when Sarah gives birth to her own son, she sends

Healing from Nonperson Status: Genesis 50:15–21

- Acknowledge the hurt — weep (v. 17).
- Leave the correcting of wrongs to God (vv. 18–19).
- See God's hand in the situation (v. 20; compare with Rom 8:28).
- Practice forgiveness (v. 21).

Hagar, with her son Ishmael, out into the desert to suffer an uncertain fate. All three of these key figures in Genesis treat others as nonpersons.

The pattern continues later in the book of Genesis. Laban treats his daughters Rachel and Leah shamefully and tricks Jacob into marrying Leah when he thinks he is marrying the one he loves, Rachel. Laban intensifies the problem by manipulating Jacob into working for another seven years with the promise that he can then have Rachel as his wife. The writer of Genesis does not moralize but simply tells the story, commenting simply that Jacob "loved Rachel more than Leah" (Gen 29:30).

Our world and churches are filled with those who know the kind of rejection and pain that Rachel and Leah most likely felt. Laban played his daughters off against each other to achieve his own financial security.

Genesis finishes with the story of Joseph, a blockbuster nonperson drama (Gen 37–50). What aggravates Joseph's brothers is the favoritism their father shows toward him. During his youthful days Joseph was the only son of Rachel, the one his father loved, whereas the other brothers were children of Leah or maidservants. Their jealousy eventually leads them to strip Joseph of his coat, throw him into a pit, and then sell him to a group of traders who take him to Egypt. Unbeknownst to

Joseph, during his years in exile in Egypt his younger brother Benjamin is born to Rachel. When Joseph's older brothers finally come to Egypt, where he ends up in a place of authority, he does not reveal his identity to them, but sends the brothers home with orders to retrieve Benjamin from Canaan and return immediately to Egypt with him (Gen 42:15–24). Throughout the story when Joseph meets his brothers he weeps uncontrollably (Gen 42:24) as he is reminded of his nonperson treatment by his own family. Joseph's story concludes with how he handles his nonperson status, as the sidebar shows.

These examples from Genesis illustrate what it looks like to treat others as nonpersons, but the gospel reverses nonperson status, declaring that in order to be right with God one must be right with one's neighbor. In Christ there is no nonperson status. The apostle Paul states in Galatians 3:28 and Colossians 3:11 that in Christ the three major forms of discrimination in his day—race, economic, gender—are overturned. Peter is slower on the uptake but finally gets the ramifications of the gospel when he meets the gentile centurion Cornelius. Peter declares: "I truly understand that God shows no partiality" (Acts 10:34).

Few understand the centrality of Jesus's resurrection to the human worth and dignity of all people. Before Paul's monumental statement in Galatians 3:28, "There is no longer Jew or Greek, there is no longer slave or free, there is no longer male and female; for all of you are one in Christ Jesus," he sets the foundation by stating, "As many of you as were baptized into Christ have clothed yourselves with Christ" (3:27). Paul is declaring here that baptism is the symbol that we have died to the old self and put on the new self. The climactic act of baptism is our identification with the risen Christ as we come out of the water. We were buried but are now raised in Christ. The way of the risen Christ is the path of human dignity and human worth for all people irrespective of race, economic status, or gender. First John affirms this idea, stating that to put on the garments of Christ is to love one's neighbor as oneself (4:7–21). The outworking of the fall in Genesis has been reversed. At the cross Jesus paid the price for our treatment of others as nonpersons and modeled true servanthood; but it is the resurrection, clothing ourselves in the risen Christ, that leads to a new day in human relationships. The resurrection is the lynchpin of God's new day for human dignity. The marks of the true church will clearly show that there is no racism, no sexism, and no socioeconomic distinctions.[90]

There are eight steps that flow from the first garden. They are interconnected. Today, the call to disciples is that in the power of the Spirit and the risen Christ we capture and exceed the blessings and commitments of the first garden, as we await the return of Jesus.

Rise!

---

90 For more examples see Clifford and Johnson, *Cross is Not Enough*, 54–63.

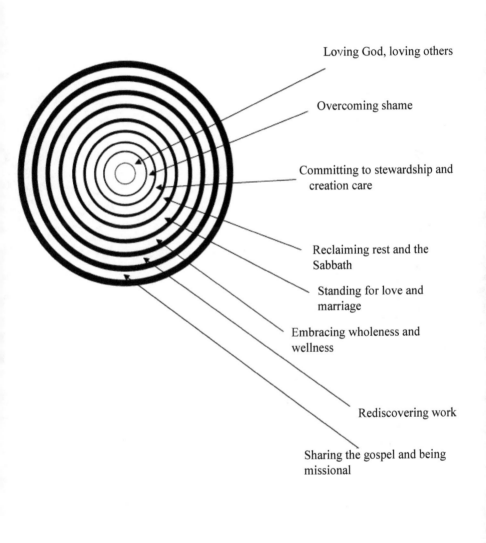

Loving God, loving others

Overcoming shame

Committing to stewardship and
creation care

Reclaiming rest and the
Sabbath

Standing for love and
marriage

Embracing wholeness and
wellness

Rediscovering work

Sharing the gospel and being
missional

BIBLIOGRAPHY

Althaus, Paul. *The Ethics of Martin Luther.* Translated by Robert
C. Schulz. Philadelphia: Fortress, 1972.

Australian Government. Department of Social Services, 2014.

Banks, Robert. *God the Worker.* Sydney: Albatross, 1992.

Banks, Robert, and Gordon Preece. *Getting the Job Done Right.*
Wheaton: Victor, 1992.

Beasley-Murray, George. *Preaching the Gospel from the Gospels.*
London: Lutterworth, 1956.

Berger, Peter L. A *Rumor of Angels.* New York: Doubleday, 1969.

Bird, Michael F. *Evangelical Theology.* Grand Rapids:
Zondervan, 2013.

Bosch, David J. *Transforming Mission.* New York: Orbis, 1991.

Bright, Jim. "Telling Your Employer You Have a Mental Illness Can Be Problematic." *The Sydney Morning Herald,* January 24–25, 2015.

Bruggerman, Walter. *Sabbath as Resistance: Saying No to the Culture of Now.* Louisville: John Knox Press, 2014.

Bynum, Caroline Walker. *The Resurrection of the Body in Western Christianity.* New York: Columbia University Press, 1995.

Calvin, John. *Commentary on Genesis, Calvin's Commentaries,* vol. 1. Translated by John King. Grand Rapids: Baker, 1999.

Campbell, Joseph, and Bill D. Moyers. *The Power of Myth.* New York: Doubleday, 1988.

Carnes, Patrick. *Don't Call It Love: Recovery from Sexual Addiction.* New York: Bantam Dell, 1992.

Chesterton, G. K. *G. K.'s Weekly,* January 29, 1928.

Ciampa, Roy, and Brian Rosner. *The First Letter to the Corinthians.* Grand Rapids, MI: Eerdmans, 2010.

Clifford, Ross, and Philip Johnson. *The Cross is Not Enough.* Grand Rapids: Baker, 2012.

Riding the Rollercoaster. Sydney, Australia: Strand, 1998.

Collins, C. *John, Genesis 1-4.* Philipsburg: P&R, 2006.

Drane, John, et al. *Beyond Prediction.* Oxford, England: Lion, 2001.

Drury, Neville. *The Shaman's Quest.* Rose Bay, NSW: Bandl and Schlesinger, 2001.

Eareckson Tada, Joni. *Heaven: Your Real Home.* Grand Rapids: Zondervan, 1995.

Eckstein, Monika, et al. "Oxytocin Facilitates the Extinction of Conditioned Fear in Humans." *Biological Psychiatry* (October 29, 2014). https://doi.org/10.1016/j.biopsych.2014.10.015.

Eliade, Mircea. "The Yearning for Paradise in Primitive Tradition." In *Myth and Mythmaking,* edited by Henry Murray, 61–75. New York: George Braziller, 1960.

Ellul, Jacques. *The Ethics of Freedom.* Grand Rapids: Eerdmans, 1976.

Ellwood, Robert. *The Politics of Myth: A Study of C. G. Jung, Mircea Eliade and Joseph Campbell.* Albany, NY: State University of New York Press, 1999.

Engstrom, Ted W. *The Pursuit of Excellence* Grand Rapids: Zondervan, 1982.

Evans, Eirena. "There's Power in the Blood." *Christianity Today* (February 2010), 38.

Foster, Tim. *The Suburban Captivity of the Church: Contextualising the Gospel for Post—Christian Australia.* Moreland, VIC: Acorn, 2014.

Garrett, Greg. *One Fine Potion: The Literary Magic of Harry Potter.* Waco, TX: Baylor University Press, 2010.

Gilbert, Elizabeth. *Eat, Pray, Love.* New York: Penguin, 2006.

Gleanings. "Why Protestants Need Rest." *Christianity Today* 59, no. 2 (March 2015), 14.

Gold, Michael. *God, Love, Sex, and Family: A Rabbi's Guide for Building Relationships That Last.* Lanham, ML: Jason Aronson, 1998.

Grisham, John. *The Testament.* New York: Doubleday, 1999.

Harris, Rich, and Claire Provost. "The Millennium Development Goals." *The Guardian,* September 24, 2014.

Hart, Ian. "The Teachings of the Puritans About Ordinary Work." *Evangelical Quarterly* 67, no. 3 (1995) 195–209.

Hathaway, Bill. "Meditation Helps Pinpoint Neurological Differences between Two Types of Love." *Yale News,* February 11, 2014.

Hawley, Janet. "The Hero's Journey." *The Sydney Morning Herald, Good Weekend Supplement,* October 14, 1995.

Hoekema, Anthony A. *The Bible and the Future.* Exeter: Paternoster, 1979.

Hume, Lynne. "Liminal Beings and the Undead: Vampires in the 21st Century." In *Popular Spiritualties,* edited by Lynne Hume and Kathleen McPhillips, 3–16. Aldershot, England: Ashgate, 2006.

Jobs, Steve. (n.d.). BrainyQuote.com. Retrieved March 11, 2015, from http://www.brainyquote.com/quotes/quotes/s/steve-jobs416859.html.

Johnson, Philip. "'Here We Go Again': Timelord Regeneration." *In Bigger On the Inside: Christianity and Doctor Who,* edited by Greg Thornbury and Ned Bustard. Lancaster, Pennsylvania: Square Halo Books, 2015.

Johnson, Philip, and John Smulo. "Reaching Wiccan and Mother Goddess Devotees." In *Encountering New Religious Movements*, edited by Irving Hexham, Stephen Rost, and John W. Morehead II, 209–25. Grand Rapids: Kregel, 2004.

Kelly, Thomas R. A *Testament of Devotion*. London: Hodder and Stoughton, 1943.

Keyworth, David. "The Socio-Religious Beliefs and Nature of the Contemporary Vampire Subculture." JCR 17 (2002) 355–70.

Kidner, Derek. *Genesis*. Leicester: Inter-Varsity Press, 1967.

Lane, Terry. *Good Weekend, Sydney Morning Herald*, August 27, 1994.

Levenson, Jon D. *Resurrection and the Restoration of Israel: The Ultimate Victory of the God of Life*. New Haven: Yale University Press, 2006.

Lewis, C. S. *God in the Dock: Essays on Theology and Ethics*. Grand Rapids: Eerdmans, 1970.

Mere Christianity. London: MacMillan, 1960.

"The Weight of Glory." *Theology* (November 1941). London: SPCK.

Matrix Reloaded. Warner Bros, 2003.

Matthews, Kenneth A. *The New American Commentary, Genesis 1–11:26*, vol. 1A. Nashville: Broadman & Holman, 2001.

McGrath, Alister. *Springboard for Faith*. London: Hodder and Stoughton, 1993.

McKenzie, Leon. *Pagan Resurrection Myths and the Resurrection of Jesus: A Christian Perspective*. Charlottesville, VA: Bookwrights, 1997.

Moltmann, Jurgen. *The Coming of God: Christian Eschatology*. Translated by Margaret Kohl. London: SCM Press, 1996.

Moyers, Bill. "Interview with George Lucas." *Time Magazine*, May 3, 1999, 71–74.

Neill, Stephen. *Christian Holiness*. Cambridge, UK: Lutterworth Press, 1960.

Ortberg, John. *Soul Keeping and Caring for the Most Important Part of You*. Grand Rapids: Zondervan, 2014.

Pascal, Blaise. *Pensees*. Translated by A. J. Krailsheimer. New York: Penguin Books, 1986.

Paul, Marla. "The Love Hormone is Two-Faced." Northwestern University, July 2013.

Russell, Jeffrey Burton. *The Prince of Darkness: Radical Evil and the Power of Good in History.* London: Thames & Hudson, 1989.

Schwartz, Barry. *The Paradox of Choice—Why More is Less.* New York: Harper Perennial, 2004.

Shead, A. G. "Sabbath." In *New Dictionary of Biblical Theology,* edited by T. D. Alexander and Brian Rosner, 745–50. Downers Grove: InterVarsity, 2003.

Sloane, Andrew. "Peace in Our Time." *CASE Quarterly 33* (2012).

Sproul, R. C. *If There is a God, Why Are There Atheists?* Minneapolis: Bethany, 1978.

Spurgeon, C. H. Sermon 3180. "Christ the Creator." *In Spurgeon's Sermons,* vol. 56 (1910), 31. Christian Classics Ethereal Library. www.ccel.org/ccel/spurgeon.

Stiles, Peter. *Resurrection Sunday, Trumped by Grace.* Mont Albert North, VIC: Poetica Christi, 2015.

Tolkein, J. R. R. "On Fairy Stories." In *Essays on Theology and Ethics.* Grand Rapids: Eerdmans, 1970.

Trenoweth, Samantha. *The Future of God.* Alexandria, NSW: Millennium Books, 1995.

United Nations Department of Economic and Social Affairs, Division for Sustainable Development. "Open Working Group Proposal for Sustainable Development Goals." http://sustainabledevelopment.un.org/sdgsproposal.html.

United States Census Bureau, 2014.

Van Dyke, Henry. "VIII, Au Large." In *Little Rivers.* New York: Charles Scribner's Sons, 1895.

Wilcox, W. Bradford, and Elizabeth Williamson. "The Cultural Contradictions of Mainline Family Ideology and Practice." In *American Religions and the Family,* edited by Don S. Browning and David A. Clairmont, 37–55. New York: Columbia University Press, 2007.

Wolterstorff, Nicholas. "More on Vocation." *The Reformed Journal* 29, no. 5 (May 1979), 20–23.

Until Justice and Peace Embrace. Grand Rapids: Eerdmans, 1983.

Wright, Bradley R. E. *Christians Are Hate-Filled Hypocrites . . . and Other Lies You've Been Told: A Sociologist Shatters Myths From the Secular and Christian Media.* Bloomington, MN: Bethany House, 2010.

Wright, N. T. *Acts for Everyone, Part 2, Chapters 13–28.* West-
minster: John Knox Press, 2007.

Wynne-Jones, Jonathan. "The Church Is Ailing—Send for Dr.
Who." *Telegraph*, May 4, 2008. http://www.telegraph.co.uk/
news/newstopics/howaboutthat/1925338/The-church-is-
ailing---send-for-Dr-Who.html.

Zongker, Brett. "AP Exclusive: Picasso Painting Reveals Hidden
Man." *Associated Press,* June 17, 2014.